Yorkshire 2027

A Strategy For Tomorrow

By Steve Mullins

Dedicated to Jonathan.
You are missed.

Contents

Note to Readers

The book is in three parts:

Part 1. – Foundation which discusses the background to the political low point somewhere between 2018 and 2023; the economy was tanking, confidence in UK politicians was at an all-time low and industry was being failed.

Part 2. – A winning Formula looks back from 2027 when there was a turning point and, in Yorkshire, society, industry and politics began to find a new balance as the County recognised a future with promise of prosperity and hope for its people. The narrative describes how a small number of organisations developed a winning strategy – a strategy that itself becomes a foundation for further growth and development, a strategy to become more widely adopted.

Part 3. – Looking Forward from 2027 at how the strategy might unfold and the balance between society, commerce and politics be redressed through economics and where all pull together for mutual benefit and even begin to think about the self-sufficiency that was the original objective.

This is the story of how these changes occurred.

Foreword

Way back in 1968 Arthur Wise published [*The Day The Queen Flew To Scotland For The Grouse Shooting*], and his quote on the back cover reads:

"... there is a great sense of frustration in the North, and a general disillusion with the central Government. I seriously believe that unless the North gets more decentralised government and wider consultation, then there will be violence".

He wrote on the last page but one *"... And nothing can change it. No one must be allowed to hold any new ideas, to see any new shape. The function of government is preservation. ... We've seen through it. It's hollow."*

As a Yorkshireman, I moved South after graduating and found it took me at least ten years to properly acclimatise to the different culture – which makes politicians' "I understand and share your feelings" as hollow now as it was in 1968.

Returning home, public transport is sporadic at best, poverty at an all-time high, wages at an all-time low and the health service falling apart.

Yet, despite the bleak conditions, and little chance of government-driven improvement in the foreseeable future, there is still hope.

I believe Arthur Wise's sentiments ring as true today as they did when I was young and argue that the mission of the North is turn things to our own advantage and social betterment.

This book explores one such option.

Introduction

For centuries there has been a sequence of: invention, expansion, regulation and documentation which is echoed in a bewildering variety of studies and provides the backdrop to the organisations that had got together and into a position to flourish by 2027.

These are the organisations that are ideally situated to grow formidably and sustainably into the 2030s, influencing society and politics as they develop and strengthen.

In my earlier book *Yorkshire, The Case for Independence,* which was published in 2020, I describe a situation that is actually feasible and could be achieved in time; this is the first step on that journey.

By 2027 there have been some small changes in the Yorkshire mindset, a transformation to organisational focus, an ability to adapt and the agility to cope with outside events.

The book is written for the Owners, Directors and Managers of Small and Medium-sized Enterprises in Yorkshire – along with their Membership Organisations – those companies that are prepared to adapt and continue to provide the jobs that generate the wealth that supports their local communities.

Enterprises that just want a fair throw of the dice.

Summary

A number of publications (see the bibliography) talk about the what – what will it all look like, feel like etc. This book begins to address the how – how will we get stronger, reduce dependency on elected politicians and actually go some way towards the magic that is 'levelling-up'.

The year is 2027; three years after an election when political bias was changed – but not enough to address the pandemonium that had been Westminster politics for the last twenty years[1].

Businesses are still struggling to make up the ground lost to Brexit, politicians were running out of excuses, banks were foreclosing or withholding loans, Yorkshire was still sidelined with any investment going to places closer to London and all the while society was getting even more polarised with increasing numbers of foodbanks and reducing numbers of opportunities.

Some organisations were getting by through the use of social media which had been described as either an 'echo chamber' or a filter bubble' which simply conveyed, or amplified, data (or at best information), and was used by some as a substitute for management but did little to promote original thinking or drive business.

---

[1] The quality of the senior politicians of the time (2016 – 2020) is very ably summed up by Alan Duncan [*In the Thick Of It*]

However, over the last few years and against this background of stagnation and deterioration, a number of frustrated organisations had broken away from relying on the political parties for support and were beginning to thrive by taking a new look at how they operated and how they related to one another. This is the story of how commerce began to overtake politics to create a better Yorkshire.

Initially, any new ideas had been derided as impractical – 'It's never been tried, so it can't work'; ideas had been sought through social media, but these ideas were, naturally, widely shared and gave little competitive edge, despite assurances (and charges!) to the contrary.

Eventually, a Yorkshire-wide Group (The Hub), that had several Trade Organisations as Participants, devised and made available a scheme whereby the Members of the Trade Organisations could come together in mutually beneficial cooperatives – if only they knew how to do this in a manner that would create a stable and sustainable union.

The average Yorkshire person is generally described as a bit dour and steady – 'if it were good enough for me dad, it's good enough for me' however, there are parts of England that are a bit more accommodating and the Hub drew on a number of precedents to bring organisations together using a process that had been shown to work elsewhere.

Looking back from 2027, organisations selected to come together cooperatively knew each other's strengths and weaknesses, having learned from the other alternative stronger business processes.

Now, in 2027, the Hub is beginning to engage larger organisations to create opportunities for the SMEs who had hitherto been frustrated in attempts to win contracts with big organisations, work often going to 'Preferred Suppliers' nominated by government and often many miles away.

Other organisations were becoming interested in how local firms were doing better than they were and began to approach the Hub, starting a movement that is destined to benefit the County as a whole, not only drawing commercial organisations together but also including academia and the creative sector.

The 2024 elections changed national politics but not enough to properly support Yorkshire, whilst the influence of the bankers in Westminster was also diverting the politicians' attention away from the people they were elected to represent.

Finally, looking ahead from 2027, there is a period of calm as Westminster prepares for the 2029 election and disgruntled peers, seeing their wealth eroded, decide to stand for Parliament (in safe seats of course). The peers' interest outside investment banking was pretty negligible and paved the way for invention, transformation and a non-classical form of economics to surface; economics that recognised society and people outside the rarefied atmosphere of the banks.

Part 1 – Foundation.
The Signs of Impending Change (2022).

Back in 2022, a significant number of commentators were projecting a substantial change to local and world events around the year 2026; and, we're now a year further on.

World events are important because, over the last 70 or so years, we have become increasingly connected; perhaps starting with Bretton Woods in 1944 when the American Dollar was accepted internationally as the currency of trade.

For many years I have refuted that 'the past is the key to the future'; however, since retiring and having the luxury of time to read and gossip I am changing my views (firm ideas loosely held). Now with the luxury of a good length of personal history and a variety of ways to join the dots between the numerous events I am now of the opinion that we can use history to (begrudgingly) give us an insight to what might be round the corner.

2022 was a turning point, a nadir, people were seriously losing faith in a complacent government that was focused on the big London banks; the economy was failing and it couldn't all be explained by Covid, Ukraine or Brexit; society was becoming increasingly unequal with conspicuous opulence on the one hand and extreme poverty, with foodbanks, on the other.

In order to set the scene, here I reproduce a letter I wrote my local newspaper and a response that came the following week:

<u>Setting the Scene.</u>

My Letter.

At the end of 2022, I wrote to the Gazette & Herald in York[2] expressing dismay at the way central government was managing the country.

Here it is:

Austerity Logic?

As we go into 2023 and look at the abysmal state of Northern infrastructure and our disadvantaged society I can only reflect on the £30bn squandered on Track & Trace, another £30bn lost through incompetent fiscal policy and yet another £30bn (or thereabouts) poured into the pockets of government cronies – a litany of staggering incompetence.

The end of 2022 has seen care workers, nurses and teachers crying for help – people who have to demonstrate a degree of competence in order to have these jobs. We are also seeing single mums and gig workers in deep distress; yet help has been denied by a bunch of incompetents on six-figure salaries with generous expense accounts who claim that we can't afford to help those people of this country who desperately need support.

Can you explain, in simple terms, the logic behind austerity?

---

[2] December 28th 2022

Putting Me Right? Or Agreeing?

The following week the letter below was published[3], recreated here section by section with my comments. It read:

Be thankful for friends and family.

Our government consists largely of privileged, intelligent, highly articulate people who have benefited from some of the best education available in the world. They are also informed by a huge array of similarly well-educated and experienced experts and advisors from every field.

Looking at the current parlous state of the country, its economy, public services, industries and many of the people, it's tempting to think that the Government is inept, incompetent and bereft of ideas, but that doesn't tally with my first paragraph.

<u>Comment</u>: I have two degrees, been Chartered and Certificated, held peer-reviewed Memberships and Fellowships, held Directorships and Partnerships, trained managers, and marked management qualifications to level 7.

Despite all this, I do not have the competence to drive a tractor or conduct an orchestra, so I challenge whether degrees in the history and theory of Philosophy, Politics & Economics, Geography or Classics delivers the competence to join the dots, make decisions or envisage outcomes from very large and complex societal situations.

---

[3] Gazette & Herald, York. 4th January 2023

Getting the degrees does, however, teach people to think and if not incompetent, then perhaps gullible or selfish?

Consequently, the only rational conclusion is that almost everything this government does is deliberate and calculated. If so, who benefits and in what way, as it doesn't appear to be the economy, public services, industries and many of its people, despite the concerted efforts of sections of the media to convince people otherwise?

<u>Comment:</u> So, not only do we have a dereliction of duty in our 'ruling' politicians we also have benefits directed away from those people the government purports to serve, which leaves themselves and the financial sector as the only remaining beneficiaries, actively supported by the (self-interested?) media.

[... despite all this we are better off than many] Here's hoping for better things in 2023 and the leadership to make it that way.

<u>Comment:</u> Hear, hear.

<u>Recent UK Political Focus</u>

It's well established that finance and politics go hand in hand, but before exploring the financial linkages it is helpful to explore how we got to this state of affairs by examining the political types who have made it to Prime Minister.

Some years ago when I was Development Manager I mapped the course an idea goes through in getting to be profitably marketed. This course (assuming acceptance at every point) followed a regular theme:

- Prototype – proves the market is there
- Rapid expansion & diversification – several variations developed, the market is flooded
- Consolidation – the more popular variants win through, are closely specified and the quality is closely regulated,
- Decline – people get bored, the competition develops something better and we all remember the original version fondly.
- Cycle restarts with a new Prototype.

This cycle is reflected in several other settings; for example, personality types and also in marketing where the customers for a product change from Early Adopter to Late Adopter through Late Majority and finally, the Laggards[4].

The mobile telephone followed this pattern, and, as shown below, UK Politics also matches this cycle!

The trends since the end of World War Two in the UK are perhaps more clearly illustrated in the succession of British Prime Ministers where there can only be one at a time and they are elected by the governing party, themselves elected by the people of the day – so presumably representative.

---

[4] Attributed to Everett M. Rogers book 'Diffusion of Innovations'

The sweeping assumption is that the individuals heading government not only reflect society, technology and industry but also direct how these are managed and legislated and, as such, provide quite a precise indicator of the Country's focus and management style as it grows and changes.

1947 – 1967 – Innovation.

Initiation – a time of energy, ideas and change refining and developing wartime developments such as radar, propulsion and communication.

Through history, many inventions, novelties and breakthroughs have been the province of:

- The Landed Gentry – Lord Kelvin.
- The Explorer – Charles Darwin.
- The Academic – Marie Curie.

Without being too unkind – these were people who had the money, space or facilities to escape the all-day drudgery of factory or farm work and instead could devote time to thinking, imagining and trialling – without fear of blame and in an atmosphere of continual learning[5].

1950 – 55. Winston Churchill (Duke of Marlborough).

1955 – 57 Anthony Eden (Earl of Avon).

1957 – 63 Harold Macmillan (Earl of Stockton).

1963 – 64 Alec Douglas-Home (Lord Dunglass).

1964 – Harold Wilson

---

5 Please see *[Nothing]*; New Scientist Pg 16ff.

This was a period that (with political detachment) saw the perfection and introduction of:

- The Thermonuclear bomb (1952).
- The hard drive (1956).
- The Birth Pill (1957) – but restricted usage.
- Jet Airliners (1958).
- Integrated circuit (1959).
- Communications Satellites (1962).
- Integrated Computer Systems (1968).
- The Arpanet (forerunner of the world-wide web) (1969).
- Fibre Optics (1970).

These inventions paved the way to develop markets and diversify; others would substantially develop these creations during the next phase.

How many people remember these inventors:

- Theodore Maiman – the laser.
- Roy Tomlinson – e-mail.
- Federico Faggin – single-chip microprocessor.

The politicians of the day were, in effect by-standers and facilitators with people pretty much left alone to get on and do things.

1967 – 1987 – Implementation.

Growth –reaping the rewards of innovation with expansion and efficiency.

The leisured political class were replaced by the hungrier commoner.

It was a period of support for industry and further development of the innovations of the previous era.

Talking to my contemporaries, this was a time of factory building, efficiency and aggressive trade, supported by Prime Ministers with a level of experience outside Westminster:

- 1970 Harold Wilson (son of an industrial chemist).
1970 – 1974 Edward Heath (a commoner).
1974 – 1976 Harold Wilson (again).
1976 – 1979 Jim Callaghan (working class).
1979 – Margaret Thatcher (Grocer's Daughter. Chemistry graduate, later qualifying as a barrister).

All were Oxford graduates, despite their working/middle class backgrounds except Jim Callaghan who couldn't afford the tuition fees so went to work for the Inland Revenue instead.

This period saw the development and exploitation of:

- Electronic ignition (1972) from the integrated circuit?
- The Cray supercomputer (1976) from integrated computer systems?
- The Personal Computer (1977) also from integrated computer systems?
- GPS (1978) from communications satellites?
- The CD (1979) from fibre optics?

There was some further innovation (but to a lesser degree) with:

- MRI (Magnetic Resonance Imaging) (1973) – integrated circuit?
- The Barcode (1974)?
- DNA fingerprinting (1984) – using integrated computer systems?

And, it might reasonably be argued that these derived substantially from earlier invention.

This was a period of significant support for industry with notable events being:

- 1973 – Britain joins the EU (growth opportunities).
- 1984 – Nissan investment in Sunderland.
- 1986 – Financial services deregulated (the big bang).

The firms and people who developed these applications generally did better than those who invented them; a clear case of not the early bird getting the worm but the second mouse getting the cheese.

With this proliferation of industry my personal view is that government felt control was being wrested from its hands and its control and influence needed to be re-established.

Next to step up to the plate are the regulators and legislators who imposed increasing control and supervision on industry (perhaps with the exception of banking – see below):

1987 – 2007 Imposition.

Regulation – a time to control the growth.

The premiership of Thatcher is quite interesting in that she started as a chemist and then became a barrister which reflected government's changing management style and paved the way for the process and procedure of the next era.

After a sad farewell, Thatcher was replaced by John Major in an era that saw the rise of the professional regulator.

...... – 1990 Margaret Thatcher (Perhaps a better chemist than Barrister?) – Ousted.

1990 – 1997 John Major (no qualifications see note below).

1997 – 2007 Tony Blair (Barrister).

<u>Note:</u> John Major's biography notes that, after qualifying as a banker, as Chief Secretary to the Treasury he was admired by colleagues for being able to keep spending down; promoted to Foreign Secretary and then Chancellor – so he evidently had significant (accountancy and control?) capabilities.

In terms of commercial development there is little of real significance during this period and although you might argue we got the World-Wide Web, Windows, Facebook, Linked-In, i-phones, and a host of operational platforms, this was nearly all further development of established technology which started with the hard drive, the integrated circuit and the Arpanet.

What is significant though is the range of (essentially non-commercial, bureaucratic) reforms brought in by government:

- Privatised British Rail.
- Reformed criminal justice.
- Scottish & Welsh devolution.
- Reform of the House of Lords.
- Freedom of Information Act.
- Good Friday Agreement.
- Intervention in Iraq.
- Public Sector reform (doubled in size).
- Bills on Foundation Hospitals.
- Bills on University tuition fees.
- Intervention in Afghanistan.
- Reduction in civil liberties.
- Codification of Prime Minister's Question Time.

This was a time when the number of public sector employees all but doubled in size; either contrary to Professor [*Parkinson's Law*] that governmental growth has a norm of about 6% p.a. regardless of the amount of work to be done, or a catch-up for the last seven years (7x6=42, pretty much a doubling).

Please see also *Peter's Principle Revisited* below at page 22.

Additionally, the school leaving age was raised and university education opened to almost anyone who could get hold of a (readily available) student loan. A seriously unproductive time but the job-seeker (i.e. dole queue) numbers went down which looked good for the various elections.

Despite the increasing magnitude of the Civil Service, nothing was done about the financial sector which had been problematic for years: 1967 Devaluation, 1973 Oil crisis & 3-day week, 1976 IMF crisis, 1980 Recession and Friedman economics, 1980 Thatcher & Regan deregulating the banks, 1986 boom-and-bust, 1992 black Wednesday (joined the ERM) and the removal of the Bank of England from government control, scrutiny and supervision in 1997 (after several years getting the legislation right) – all of which should have signalled some sort of problem – a problem which came at us headlong in 2008.

This was a time of increasing regulation and bureaucracy, for all but the banks carried through to the next set of ministers.

2007 – Implosion.

Reporting A time to reflect on the extent of control, a time of procrastination.

The country's leaders evolved from the professional class to the observational class –
loads of theory, some abstract analysis and not much practical capacity or life in the real world.

2007 – 2010 Gordon Brown (PhD Historian).

2010 – 2016 David Cameron (Direct from Oxford University to Conservative Research).

2016 – 2019 Theresa May (Banking & Clearing)

2020 – 2022 Boris Johnson (Journalist).

2022 – 2022 Liz Truss (Disruptive, several papers, continual shifting of departments).

2022 – 2024 Rishi Sunak, (Investment Banker) trying to get the Conservatives re-elected in 2024 by providing impressive-sounding grants that didn't really stack up when analysed.

The big event was in 2008 when the investment bankers eventually exploded the financial sector, but not until 2016 was there any (inadequate) 'stress testing' and there is still no adequate financial control. The dynamics of the financial crash that wrecked many lives around the world are still in evidence.

- Numerous take-overs of UK industry (mainly by US investment funds) which has resulted in their being 'hollowed out' and the remains sold on; but more of this later.

- A check in 2020 showed something like 30% of audits by the 'Big Seven' were substandard; in 2021 there is talk (and little else) of giving the Financial Standards Authority a new name (some new teeth as well might have helped).

- Iraq had been invaded and we still look on. There was little or no strategy or planning but plenty of news coverage and still little help for those Iraqis who sided with the UK.

- Facebook and other platforms were launched and continue to allow 'hate mail', 'fake news' and personal intrusion, still with no adequate policing, despite a pretences at regulation in other countries as well as the UK.

- North African and Arabian wars are still on-going with little action to resolve them but regular reports that tell us little.
- Malala Yousafazi won the Nobel Prize for struggles against the suppression of childrens' rights. Rights that are still suppressed (as are womens' rights).
- Companies 'hollowed out' by private equity firms, with UK jobs going to China; unlike the earlier Nissan investment that actively brought jobs and supported the local community.
- The Equality Act 2010 which generated 'Equality Impact Assessments' – themselves often works of egregious fiction, reinforcing their writers' journalistic tendencies.
- Brexit is still unresolved but lots of meetings, warm words and endless reports keep kicking the can down the road; the Northern Ireland Accord still being debated several years later.
- A succession of 'climate accords' promising much but delivering little. Reported in 2020 that China has commissioned two new fossil fuel generating plants to be built!
- Given that our politicians have done so little that's actually productive there is not much criticism that could be useful or meaningful.
- And then there's Donald Trump – and the world spectated.

In every case noted above, those who could have acted didn't, people suffered and the various trends were allowed to take root and continue to flourish.

<u>Twenty Years B.S.</u>
Ten years of events and some parallels:
(For Americans, – *B.S means Before Steve*)

Then: 1928 - 1938, the Great Depression.
      Now: 2008-2018, the Great Financial Crash.

Then: Extreme poverty and homelessness.
      Now: Poor get poorer (but with social
          support).

Then: Radio the favoured mass communication
      medium.
      Now: Social media most favoured.

Then: Germany builds warships & planes.
      Now: Armaments growth in totalitarian
      countries.

Then: Floods and wild weather.
      Now: Floods, fires and wild weather.

Then: Physical war with ships, guns and bombs.
      Now: Cyber wars with currency,
          surveillance & personal data.

It all looks a bit repetitive and familiar!

Except for the Prime Ministers: Stanley Baldwin, Neville Chamberlain (who seemed to dislike education and spent time in the family business) and Ramsay MacDonald (who maintained a keen interest in Scottish politics).

Might it be concluded that they were just detached observers – a bit like the writers and journalists of Parliament over the last 20 years?

The indications are that we are about to enter a new era of innovation as earlier developments by now have been pushed, more-or-less, to their limits and the time is right to begin to link developments and research together to open new boundaries and realise new opportunities.

Peter's Principle[6] Revisited.

As stated by L. J. Peter. His principle is that as individuals rise through the increasingly complex layers of management in an organisation their job eventually becomes too big for them, at which point they become ineffective (incompetent?)

Let's now turn this principle on its head and examine whether there's a situation where layers can get added to the person (or position) until the weight and complexity gets a bit much and, Lo and Behold, Westminster 1997 – 2007 (*Imposition*).

---

[6] From Wikipedia: "The Peter principle is a concept in management developed by Laurence J. Peter, which observes that people in a hierarchy tend to rise to "a level of respective incompetence": employees are promoted based on their success in previous jobs until they reach a level at which they are no longer competent, as skills in one job do not necessarily translate to another."

It may be argued that, as the level of power and authority has imperceptibly continued to aggregate around an ever-diminishing No.10 Cabinet with ever-growing egos, the level of competence of the various Prime Ministers and cabinet members might have remained fairly constant but the complexity of the job has continued to grow to a point where those charged with delivering a result (some without any semblance of work experience or appropriate training) might be considered to have reached the point of incompetence.

This perceived incompetence appears to have bred a degree of paranoia that reflects badly on a me-first ego (poor decisions might get found out) and leads to a culture of blame and retribution; but, more importantly, others are not allowed to make decisions in case someone else's poor decision reflects on that large (but fragile) ego.

Over the last few decades, government decisions have taken longer to be reached, must follow precise and increasingly detailed rules to shield ministers from potential error and involve rising numbers of people to check each other's work.

This narrow interpretation of government regulations removed humanity from decision-making; rarely more evident than in the early 2020s with asylum seekers being processed too slowly or deported, interpreters in the middle-eastern wars denied entry to the UK because, technically, they weren't working directly for government and the Ghurkhas and other overseas troops who supported the UK being denied pension rights and rights of entry. Shameful behaviour.

Additionally, this mentality has gradually eroded the decision-making in the regions – a stand-out example from childhood is that our councils can no longer pass bye-laws – rules and regulations particular to the locality and its needs.

And so our local and regional political leaders have become increasingly hamstrung and all but ineffectual.

No Progress Without Crisis?

In commerce, *Form Follows Function*; if we want to do something novel or different we get on with it and design the administration, controls and quality systems around the new, or amended, 'thing'.

In government the opposite appears to be the case, in that *Function Follows Form* – if there isn't already in place an existing system of administration (bureaucracy), then it can't be done.

This inertia seems to be the stuff of politics and is the antithesis of good management.

Good management, on the other hand shows that the astute manager, given a challenge, will employ someone better than themself, participate in the solution and experience all the things that go right and wrong, learning from the experience.

More recently (since a bit after 1987) The astute (inept?) politicians seem to have surrounded themselves with people who are less competent than they are and can blame those people for failure; thereby reinforcing the dictum that the status quo is a good place to be.

Part of this reinforcement can be seen in the politicians' use of policy – an intention[7] that can be put into law – and changed at a stroke!

Whereas in commerce the driver is strategy – a means to meet a SMART Objective that fulfils a need with a benefit. Strategy is very difficult to change and can't be put into law.

The one can be manipulated, the other can't; and, politicians not having clear strategy means there are no clear plans – whenever we hear about a plan (or a 'roadmap') there is never anything tangible provided to give it life – other than perhaps continual reminders about sums of money (our money!)

I leave it up to you to make up your own mind as to the various levels of competence and, instead of providing further opinionated commentary, point to Alan Duncan's book [*In the thick of it*] that documents the aptitude and character type of the various senior politicians who were active between 2016 and 2020 – surely the nadir of British politics.

---

[7] Lots of debate, meetings, committees, fine print and points of order.

<u>Money</u>

Money is the glue that binds people, politics and commerce together. What is less obvious is that money comes in two forms:

- We have *Societal Money*[8] (notes and coins in circulation plus savings) which moves between people – we work, we get paid, we spend and, if we're very lucky, get to save; this represents only about 5% of all money.
- The other 95% is made up of *Fiat*[9] *Money* – bonds, government debt, mortgages – all created at the stroke of a pen and raised through the happy medium of *The Fractional Reserve* for you and me and through *Quantitative Easing* (a euphemism) for government and which also relies on a *Fractional Reserve.* or the Required Reserve Ratio (RRR)

It is perhaps worth noting here that Margaret Thatcher described budgeting along the lines of household management (societal money) and seemed to overlook fiat money (but then no-one would stand up to her and correct her thinking).

---

[8] I have adopted the expression *Societal Money* for the money circulating throughout society as a means to separate it from *fiat* money. This is not strictly accurate because credit cards, for example, generate *fiat* money; however, it is an adequate term for the development of the argument.

[9] Let there be – cf. fiat lux, let there be light.

In 1986 she then teamed up with the US president of the time, a cowboy actor called Ronald Reagan and between them they deregulated the financial markets in London and the US. Markets that ultimately gave us Nick Leeson, The 'Whale' and the 2008 debacle that ruined so many lives around the globe.

Politicians are advised by experts in neo-classic economics; advice which includes: trickle-down, rational agents, normal distributions and a macro-economy that is stable. <u>But, it excludes money</u>!

'... *when the mainstream had long ago convinced itself that the macroeconomy could* and indeed should *be modelled as if money, banks and debt did not exist*[10] '

– all fed to politicians by people who can't change their misguided tunes because these teachings are what gave them their knighthoods and professorships in the first place[11].

<u>Financial Dynamics.</u>

Additionally, to the different types of money there is a need to recognise three major types of bank – outside the Bank of England, these three types are:

---

[10] Steve Keen [*Can we avoid another...*] Pg.51

[11] There's a parallel here with Copernicus, whose work was suppressed for about 50 years, until the various intransigent clerics had retired or died.

Retail banks (clearing banks) which are present in ever-diminishing numbers on our High Streets and what most of us recognise as guardians of our money and payers of minimal interest.

Investment banks, usually attached to clearing banks and using your (appropriated) money – see below – to play in the casino that is the stock market.

Merchant banks which may be family owned and are focused on commerce and profit – even at the expense of society, or their customers.

The Retail Banks

Within the banking system there exists the *Fractional Reserve* which is the relatively small amount that must be held as assets (societal money) to justify the loans a bank creates (Fiat Money) – on the basis that not all users of the bank will withdraw their savings simultaneously, and so the bank's total liabilities can be (safely!) greater than its total assets (tell that to Northern Rock).

A similar delusion is *Quantitative Easing* which is the imaginary money created by the Bank of England based on all the clearing banks' fractional reserves and is the tool politicians have used since about 1980 (when the banks were de-regulated) as the means to cover appalling management – Test & Trace being a good example, and we might also add HS2 and various vanity bridges, runways and tunnels.

And now, here's an interesting twist, when you make a deposit with a bank; in law, that money you deposited becomes the property of the bank, otherwise it could not be added to the balance sheet to grow the bank's fractional reserve or support the quantitative easing that is yet more imaginary money to bail out the incompetence that is central government.

This process has been well documented by Mitch Feierstein as a *Ponzi Scheme* which is summarised at Appendix 1

The Investment Banks

The money that you have deposited with the banks (which has now become their property) can be multiplied by the fractional reserve and legally used to place bets on the stock market or aggregated by the Bank of England to support quantitative easing.

And, in another interesting twist, the imaginary money that is lent to central government by the Bank of England, to hide their inadequacies as managers of the economy, is structured to attract interest payments – paid in societal money; money paid from wages and trade by taxation.

The wealthy banks create imaginary money which, in turn, continues to draw societal money from those that are struggling to pay their everyday expenses; aided and abetted by the government!

And so the misguided continue to lead the gullible into deeper and deeper pointlessness.

A fraud of gargantuan proportions which continues without let or hindrance because the politicians benefit from the stock market and the bankers donate handsomely to party funds.

The Merchant Banks

Merchant banks[12] will lend to organisations that are almost certain to do well. The investments are normally at high rates of interest, around the credit card level or beyond.

This is not really a loan but a purchase of equity and the way the 'loan' works is that the capital element (equity) is paid down (bought back) by an agreed proportion each month by the company; plus an interest element. The repayment part is quite interesting in that:

- Monthly interest repayments are based on the original loan, not the diminishing sum as the investment is repaid.
- In the event of difficulty in repaying the loan there may be a 'ratchet' where the difference between the agreed repayment and what is affordable is paid in additional equity.

---

[12] The old story goes" A retail banker lends you an umbrella, then demand it back when it rains. A merchant banker lends you an umbrella and when it rains you can keep it – because it wasn't theirs anyway.

- The equity is valued at the price of the company when the loan was agreed, not its increasing value as the company grows.
- It is not unusual for the lender to insist on an 'informal advisor[13]' backed by an 'informal agreement' with the merchant bank that this advisor's instruction must be followed come-what-may (and at conflict with a shadow directorship, which it is really).
- The 'advisor, to everyone's surprise, turns out to be quite inept, giving rubbish advice that has to be followed and whilst costs go up revenue comes down and the full amount of monthly interest and equity buy-back cannot be afforded.
- The shortfall in interest and capital is paid in additional equity as per the agreed ratchet.
- Once the lender reaches 75% of the equity they effectively own the company; at which point:
    - The original Managing Director is fired.
    - The inept 'advisor' suddenly becomes clever and quite astute.
    - Sales go back up.
    - Costs come back down.
- After a period of 'settling in', the organisation gets dressed up for sale which is probably a pre-ordained purchase by a friend of the bank.

---

[13] This is very different from a shadow director in that, unlike the shadow director, the 'advisor' has no responsibility in law for how the organisation is run.

The merchant bank makes a killing! – not only on the exorbitant interest but also their increased share of the company, the growth in value of the equity, brand value, and any intellectual property.

Bringing politics and finance together.

As an example, there are regular delays and hold-ups on the A64 – a main arterial road joining east and west Yorkshire. So-called progress over the last 35 years has been: studies, reports, analyses, meetings, working parties, special interest groups, public awareness events, focus groups, more public consultations and feedback sessions with numerous detailed plans which were shelved[14] or replaced by various punts into the long grass.

For very many years this sub-standard infrastructure has not been seen in Westminster as a crisis, but as an expensive problem – and, as we all know, problems left long enough go away – don't they.

Despite commitments to taking decisions, moving some control away from Westminster, levelling-up, providing funding and reducing bureaucracy (Cameron's one-in-one-out), all we saw after eight years of promises was the tip of an iceberg when it came to dealing with expensive 'problems'.

---

[14] See: https://www.sabre-roads.org.uk/forum/viewtopic.php?t=31512

The decision-making balance had been for several decades too strongly managed by the London politicians and needed to move from London to local society and commerce.

A Need to Rebalance.

The London Financial Market contributes only 8.3% of UK GDP but is heavily supported by the Westminster elite. Manufacturing is twice this figure (17.4%)[15] but largely overlooked; the rest is agriculture and service industry – the service sector is supported to some extent by manufacturing (catering, security, janitorial etc.) which, if taken into account, would represent a more significant manufacturing sector than currently recognised.

Whilst we are governed by an elite which personally benefits from various investment instruments, their bias to the financial sector is exacerbated by a system that also hides, or covers up, their mistakes (e.g. quantitative easing) and at the same time continues to provide funds and support to the various political parties.

This support is evidenced whenever a politician is asked about strategy or management, they responded with the sums of money thrown at the situation in the hope that it would go away; none of the fundamental ***management*** issues over the last fifteen years were resolved with money, and so the bubble just got bigger and bigger.

---

[15]commonslibrary.parliament.uk/research-briefings/sn06193/

Even now, this fiat bubble is still growing, diverting attention away from the politicians – those very people who were elected to represent the best interests of their constituencies – a bubble that will continue to divert attention away whilst the following situations persist in government:

- Significant residual debt hiding bad management.
- Selection of ministers unable (incapable or unwilling) to challenge the person in charge.
- Easy access to quantitative easing (see also Appendix 1 – **Ponzi)**
- New debt still used to hide bad management.
- An inability by politicians to learn, instead of blame.
- A public sector workforce that sticks rigidly to prescribed rules to avoid the possibility of making a 'wrong' (blameworthy) decision.
- An unwillingness by economists to recognise money.
- Bankers' continuing support for political parties.
- A system where bankers and politicians (and broadcasters?) have similar backgrounds and educations with little outside experience and who hob-nob and attend each other's exclusive social events.
- A bureaucracy that discourages innovation or change.
- The status quo used as a blame-free place to maintain excessive bureaucracy and hide.

<u>Trade Deals.</u>

Manufacturing realistically comprises about 35% of British GDP and seems to be an area least understood by those in Westminster.

This lack of understanding may be exemplified by a few examples:

- The Brexit debacle that cost the country something like 4% of GDP (equivalent to three years' normal growth – every year!) but did not affect the banking industry.
- The 2021 so-called Free Trade Agreement with Australia where the UK agreed to:
    - Remove export duties on 99% of Australian goods into the UK – $9.2bn (£5bn).
    - Remove $43m of customs duties on Australian wine.
    - Remove tariffs on beef, sheep, sugar and seafood.
    - Make it easy for Australian firms to bid for UK contracts.

Yet, there was no reciprocal Free Trade Agreement for UK goods into Australia as of 2023.

Industrial and Commercial businesses (many of which are involved in trade) contribute about 75% of UK corporation tax and employ about 27m people.

Finance and Life assurance contribute about 20% and the banks plus offshore only 4%[16]

Yet despite industry and commerce contributing nearly three times as much to the UK treasury's coffers and providing livelihoods for twenty times as many people, the government continues to de-regulate the banks, fight the unions and impose 'austerity' on the rest of us.

Hitherto, changing the government's focus has never been more than a pipe-dream.

Business in 2022.

There is a neat division between **Monetary Policy** which is under the control of the banks who decide how much to issue and who to issue it to, and **Fiscal Policy** which is the responsibility of the government who decide what to do with the money and where it might be best spent.

And it's <u>not</u> being spent where it matters – with businesses that are an integral part of society, infrastructure or public services outside London.

By 2022, politicians' rhetoric is being recognised for what it really is – so much unsubstantiated claptrap peddled to a largely unsuspecting public through compliant broadcasters in order to hang on to imaginary power and misplaced influence.

---

[16]https://www.gov.uk/government/statistics/corporati on-tax-statistics-2021/corporation-tax-statistics-commentary-2021

This centralisation of power and influence has drained the regions and damaged society.

In an effort to hang on to their dwindling small businesses, the small business owners were cutting costs, reducing hours and diminished their service levels.

There was also a retreat by the various banks when lending to smaller organisations was reduced; additionally, to cover themselves in case of clients defaulting on their existing loans, interest levels were increased to provide the necessary 'cushion' to ensure the banks' continuing profitability as their clients foundered.

Some Growing Trends

Despite all the doom and gloom noted above, there was enough happening at home and abroad to give hope in the future and confidence to adapt as new knowledge became available.

Some of the changing circumstances are noted below:

UK Local Politics.

The safe public sector jobs for life with a nice pension are coming to an end and some very bright people becoming available for other work in voluntary and commercial organisations.

A degree of acclimatisation was needed by these people (and their new bosses) who, after accepting a commercial setting, became very valuable in using their experience to expand and develop organisations' core offerings, raise their customer profile and strengthen internal controls.

Society.

Over the last fifteen years weak governance and growing inequality has led to organisations banding together for some sort of security, organisations such as community support, charities and on-line groups. This inequality led to increased mental health problems and greater lawlessness where those without are stealing from those who have.

Business.

The major commercial organisations focused almost entirely on ever-increasing shareholder dividends which led to reduced investment in both business and staff with a reduction in quality and service and an erosion of customer confidence.

Technology.

US technology is responding to China's possible aggression by investing in factory building to bring militarily sensitive products and sub-components back under strict US control.

Artificial Intelligence (A.I.), coupled with the *Internet of Things* has supported technologists in developed a bewildering array of applications that increased security, gave control-at-a-distance and enhanced productivity.

A.I. also became a wonderful technology with which to influence industry, politics and society both positively and also (unfortunately) negatively.

Social Media

Social media [*You are what you read*] is a flow of unchecked material shared between like-minded people and, as such, can be biased, unresearched, quite polarised and extreme, there are reports of social media building coteries of extremists who fuel one another's biased thinking.

There are always two sides to a story and the wise organisations will check out several sources of information around any one opportunity.

There have been, and still are, attempts at putting some sort of legal boundaries to social media but all are failing; possibly because laws are country-specific and social media are globally pervasive.

<u>Other Developments</u>

In addition to electronic technology opening new possibilities there were several other major developments to build on, these include:
- "Green" technology and how energy can be created from renewable resources.
- Chemical technology developing new products that deliver benefits better.
- Physics technology: fluid flow for example still offered opportunities for renewable energy.
- Light technology e.g. speeding up crop development.
- Magnetic devices for safe low-energy delivery.
- Nuclear fusion has started to become a reality.
- Cyclical Economics with components designed to be re-purposed.
- Biological technology.
- Plant disease management.
- Medical technology.
- Artificial Intelligence to live longer, better.

All these developments opened opportunities to 'recycle' experience and knowledge as part of the up-coming programme of investment and provided new production and training openings for older, experienced people.

<u>Summary Of The Core Considerations.</u>

- Invest in assets that not only support today's business but also support expansion and diversification.
- Be prepared to trade in more than one currency.
- Acknowledge what is happening globally and implications for suppliers and customers as well as yourself.
- Don't trust politicians.
- Have several routes to market.
- Be patient if you hire ex-public sector employees.
- Maintain generous impressed stock levels.
- Keep a level of production capacity in-house.
- Don't be totally reliant on cheap overseas manufacture.
- Have more than one supplier, buy from each one and ensure each has the capacity to supply if one fails to deliver.
- Be aware enough and agile enough to change suppliers at short notice.
- Consider (and employ) a range of different sources of energy.
- Protect (and step up) physical and on-line security.
- Keep close to US technology.
- Keep close to Asian technology.
- Make optimum use of Artificial Intelligence.
- Know Artificial Intelligence well enough to stay secure.
- Use social media but critically verify any important information.

- Stay in contact with older people who still have the technical skills used by overseas suppliers.
- Ensure staff are trained for your future opportunities.
- Consider supply-chain logistics alongside cost of manufacture and availability of raw materials.

Naturally, some mistakes were made and some decisions (in hindsight) were wrong; however, the winning organisations had recognised that these were opportunities to learn, not cause for blame.

> **Note:** It's all very well to learn lessons; however, these lessons need developing into understanding.
>
> The winners were those organisations that applied this new understanding to their organisations in a tangible, practical and cooperative manner.

Bringing all this together was perhaps more readily achieved in Yorkshire than elsewhere, when you can consider Yorkshire not just as a County but also as a state of mind.

Some Global Concerns Leading to 2027

Weather.

Despite the promises and pledges made at the various COP summits, the major polluting countries are taking little meaningful action and by now, a number of major cities are under threat of flooding as the Arctic, the Antarctic and glaciers have melted more quickly that the deniers had predicted.

The impact has been to make future international trade with some countries more uncertain, for example Indonesia and the surrounding area could be barely habitable with shipping and warehousing increasingly difficult and expensive.

Migration.

Contrary to popular economics and political rhetoric, migration can be a very good thing, bringing novel approaches, new talent and a desire to belong [*Good Economics for Hard Times*]. The integration and learning from other cultures and how they do business brought the more open-minded organisations an increasingly competitive edge and both tangible and intangible benefits.

The UK government is denying migration which leads to a shortage of some skills and capabilities; it is anticipated a more liberal approach will be taken soon as a prelude to the 2024 General Election.

And Don't Overlook Academia.

Opportunities for alternative products and pure research into advanced technologies have been realised in the universities where a number of astute businesses offer not only support with invention, but also their facilities to develop these new findings commercially.

Academics readily share information as a matter of course, so the various commercial organisations take care to ensure confidentiality with enforceable non-disclosure agreements to ensure subsequent opportunities for patents and future income.

Global Politics & The Butterfly Effect.

All organisations, whatever their size, are impacted in some way by global events where *a disturbance in one place can create major disruption elsewhere.*

For Yorkshire, the various wars and skirmishes all around the globe provide opportunities to supply commercial and domestic equipment to those counties which were recovering and had a need for things like boilers, vehicle components and pharmaceuticals, plus the skills and expertise to install and maintain this equipment.

The US Elections.

The manipulation of social media had led to significant polarisation in the American people which led to the weakening of US governance and disruption by strikes, blockades and the dollar losing international strength.

China's Shifting Priorities.
China's priorities changed in the early 2020s in order to try to stave off recession, it moved from industry and low-cost manufacture to that of a more global and expansionist policy.

Emphasis changed away from manufacturing components at low cost for western businesses that had been 'hollowed out' in the interests of profit. These businesses needed to re-think their business models and consider domestic manufacture.

The Rise of Brazil.
Brazil has been increasing its low-tech manufacturing and assembly capacity, becoming an alternative source for cheap manufacture and hungry for new additional business.

Indonesia and Surrounding Countries.
Their proximity to an expanding China makes any long-term commitments suspect; additionally, opportunities for a short-term 'fix' will be subject to disruption caused by the impact of global warming (see *weather* below).

<u>Additional Considerations.</u>

There have been a number of concerns over the last few decades that have been becoming more significant. Some are summarised here:

- Finance: Internationally strong currencies (e.g. the US dollar) have become less acceptable as other nations, such as China or the Middle-East loosen their dependency on the west.
- Weather: Climate change will not go away and, despite the suffering and misery, will open opportunities in a wide range of commercial areas.
- Empire: Countries have sought to expand their influence ever since the beginning of history; technology made this easier by helping some territories grow whilst making others more insular and paranoid.
- Patents and copyrights had been brazenly exploited overseas and now as technology, for example, has become more complex it makes sound commercial sense to keep the intellectual property safely at home.
- Quality and delivery from overseas became less reliable as staff working for these cheaper manufacturers grew richer; manufacturers needed to reduce material and distribution costs to be able to pay staff the new wage levels expected.

How Change Came About.

Throwing Off the Politicians' Rhetoric

By 2027 we had had several decades of politicians avoiding decisions but trying to sound plausible and as if they were actually on the point of reaching a decision.

Before moving on to explore how organisations won through and flourished it is a salutary exercise to begin to understand how the politicians worked – if only because this will surface again and again as they try to regain a foothold and increase their power and influence; but with little substance to back up their proclamations.

The delivery of the politicians' claptrap is perhaps summarised below from three publications in particular:
[*Trust Us We're Experts*],
[*99%*] and
[*Can we avoid another financial crisis?*]

To summarise; the particularly salient points from the first of these publications [*Trust us ...*] relates to politicians' assurances that they know what they're doing and maintain their position by hiding behind a particular series of tactics which tend to follow personality types.

Some time ago I identified four types of politician; these types of people include:

- The ***Control Freak*** starves the organisation of real information and might use instead <u>vague testimonials</u>, emotionally written and with a minimum of information; the alternative is to keep everybody subservient by <u>spreading uncertainty</u> and generating fear.
- The ***Flooder*** provides too much information – often hiding contentious issues and might use <u>glittering generalities</u> along the lines of 'of course everybody knows...', or alternatively boarding the <u>bandwagon of a noisy ginger group because</u> 'this is what *everybody* wants'; when there is little evidence and even less substance.
- The ***Diverter*** readily changes direction to something easier or less politically sensitive and might use a technique called '<u>the transfer</u>', answering a different question to the one posed, or <u>calling in the uninformed to contribute</u> – because this what the 'plain folks' want, again little evidence and less substance.
- The ***Muddier*** <u>generates conflicting evidence</u> to avoid a decision, or give the option to choose the decision of the moment; this individual might use <u>loose words</u> that can later be interpreted differently, <u>or the soundbite</u> to draw attention to the trivial and away from the important or contentious.

Some Misconceptions Laid Bare

In addition to evasive rhetoric there is a tendency to throw facts about as if they have been properly researched and could provide the foundation for something significant.

There are numerous examples ranging from (so-called) academic papers through recorded speeches on platforms such as YouTube to vanity projects and empty promises including:

- Brexit – we'd all be better off.
- Levelling-up – whatever that meant.
- HS2, various bridges and runways.

From [99%] Mark Thomas describes a series of falsehoods that have passed into political rhetoric:

- *1 Profligate governments were the cause of the Eurozone crisis – wrong.*

The cause was the global financial sector speculating on an industrial scale and getting it wrong; governments can be held to account for not regulating effectively.

- *2. Austerity leads to growth – wrong.*

Very reputable research has shown that austerity is contractionary not inflationary (as shown by the Greek reduction in structural balance by 15% starting in 2007 and its economic collapse in 2015 when the country defaulted on international debt).

- *3. There is an unprecedented level of government debt – Wrong.*

The *quantitative easing* has gone almost exclusively to the top 5% and is paid for by the bottom 95% with little going to investment in the regions. Britain's most successful eras were with high debt to GDP ratios.

It may be argued that the deployment of the debt is more important than the size of it, and could lead to a genuine levelling-up for example.

And from [*Can we avoid...*] Steve Keen explodes a number of models taught in university and adopted by governments; these include:

- *Dynamic Stochastic General Equilibrium* (DSGE) models which purport to reflect macroeconomic activity and have been described as using "incredible identifying assumptions to reach bewildering conclusions" (Paul Romer) driven by unobservable fictions that Romer likens to 'phlogiston[17]'.

- *Macroeconomics,* as taught is derived from aggregated(?) microeconomics, when complexity is a more realistic driver – but apparently too difficult for main stream economists.

---

[17] https://paulromer.net/the-trouble-with-macro/WP-Trouble.pdf, page 4

- Additionally, *established economic models* ignore private debt when they are used to describe finance; they also *ignore money* – because it's just a veil over the various transactions (tell that to Sainsburys)!

Part 2. 2027 – A Winning Formula

<u>2027 Moving Forward</u>

Decisions are still blocked or delayed by a civil service trying to shake off a culture of blame and determined to stick to rules and procedures. As of 2027, there has been some progress made in moving from blaming to learning there is unlikely to be much real progress for years to come.

Unfortunately today, the economy has not recovered sufficiently from decades of mismanagement to be confident of any proposed changes sticking, and it would be folly to expect government (and in particular the civil service) to make any substantive decisions on behalf of anyone outside their masters' elite circle of bankers and wealthy chums – potentially subjecting themselves to not only the established Westminster bullies but also the sensationalist media in its various forms.

Only a crisis such as Covid, ten years ago, caused the government to move, make decisions and act in the interests of the people it purports to serve – and then belatedly.

As an example, a T.V. lecture that has not been repeated (!) was given by one of the doctors who developed the Covid vaccine when she describes a lack of funding, having to draw money from other projects in order to keep going and working 16-hour days.

Only when success was pretty much guaranteed was the funding put back in place and the other projects could re-start.

Yet, politicians still tell us about how they fully understand the situation, its urgency' how they actively supported this research and what far-sighted people they are – balderdash.

And the doctors & technicians who were desperate for funding, having fought the politicians' stifling intransigence for all those months are still not recognised.

This particular lecture appears to have been 'lost' by the BBC who seem to be pretty much a government lackey despite their professed impartiality – perhaps something to do with cronyism and license fees.

A Beacon of Hope?

The twists and turns by the UK Conservative Party over the last two decades were exposed in the 2024 election when the Labour Party actually got a grip and properly stated the reasons for the last 40 years of economic muddle.

The origin was in Margaret Thatcher and Ronald Regan de-regulating the investment banks (Conservative decisions) which opened the floodgates to profligate speculation, growth in private debt and the description of the stock market as a casino.

The Conservative (Casino?) Party had managed to convince everyone that the 2008 debacle had been caused by Labour's shortcomings when, in fact, it had been caused by global activity following the Conservative and American deregulation.

But for years Labour had rolled over and accepted this misleading narrative[18]. At last they were beginning to wake up and look at how things had actually developed and the history-books manipulated.

Classical economics is beginning to be shown up as seriously out of touch, share dealings were moving out of London and the banks were becoming more prepared to lend to entrepreneurs and less prepared to speculate on the imaginary values of stocks and shares.

<u>Nationally.</u>

The cultural divide between north and south has led to both tensions and opportunities. The north-south divide with the lack of financing and all that goes with weak investment is well documented; perhaps less well documented is the demographic divide where Millennials are getting private and family funds to develop ideas and business opportunities as elderly relatives pass on.

---

[18] Please see *Steve Keen* Can we avoid another financial crisis? Pp89-95

<u>Other Helpful Events</u>

- Academia is working more closely with industry to give students greater practical experience as technology etc. gets increasingly complex and, paradoxically, adaptable.
- After the 2024 election, Northern Labour seats that had gone to Conservative went back to Labour amplifying the northern voice in Westminster.
- The deserted industrial sites and brown field provided land and buildings to re-develop strategic heavy engineering such as turbines and railway lines.
- Local developments in technology supported cheaper small-scale manufacture which brought Chinese-manufactured components or products[19] back to the UK.
- The increased opportunities to manufacture; whilst now cheaper; provided opportunities for greater levels of employment (mainly in the north – traditionally, a manufacturing region).
- The need by heavy industry and others for sub-contractors, specialists and local suppliers supported the SMEs who, banded together, began to create a significant presence in the North.

---

[19] Components or products that had been made in China so that the major manufacturers could 'hollow out' their companies and keep their dividends growing (known in some circles as Zombie Organisations).

<u>Bringing it all Together.</u>

A good number of influences and events (the threads) have been discussed in the main narrative; naturally, a number of these threads were more relevant than others in supporting our road to independence.

The more relevant ones are discussed below and then brought together into a coherent picture of how we not only survived the politicians but thrived in spite of them.

Some Positive Threads.

<u>For the County:</u>

Additional characteristics are described in [*Yorkshire The Case For Independence*]. The more relevant traits are summarised below:

- A history and surplus of agriculture and primary extraction.
- The UK's region of creativity and invention stretching back to the industrial revolution.
- A legacy of earning through manufacturing industry and adding tangible/real value (turning lumps of metal into tools and cars).
- Deep-water ports.
- Tenacity and thrift (or as some would have it stubbornness and meanness).

A New Industrial Revolution.

Another industrial revolution started in the North around 2025, driven this time by the smaller organisations and not by the likes of Richard Arkwright or Titus Salt.

The financial markets have had their time of influence and their power base (London) is gradually moving overseas for stability, leaving the politicians a bit out of touch because few of them have hands-on experience of industry, profit responsibility or delivering benefits.

It's the smaller, privately owned organisations that are now beginning to make their presence felt, and here's how it happened.

A Winning Formula Emerges

With new knowledge comes the ability to adapt.
Dick Stroud[20]

What was found to be possible was a change to the mind sets of local commercial enterprises to work more closely and harmoniously together; this brought substantial social change, greater prosperity and, as a consequence the potential to influence political decisions well into the future.

---

[20] The Joy of Moaning

<u>Making a Start.</u>

The key concept is that of clustering – go into a town and the restaurants are in the same area; similarly for banks and shops.

Some regions are noted for their collective skills: Sheffield for steel, Clydeside for ships and biotech in and around Cambridge.

The Yorkshire Winners were those organisations that were open-minded, prepared to innovate, ensure staff were appropriately and adequately trained, and whose clustering was based on complementary strengths, not location.

The analogy I have used is one of a ball of cotton wool – we all have connections, some permanent (family) some transitory (the darts team) and some virtual (social media); the places where connections come together (gatherings) no longer need to be physical and can be thought of as knots in the cotton wool – they can occur anywhere and at any time; some permanent, some transitory.

Imagine these knots as businesses that actually make greater use of their connections and with more open communication[21] – complementing each other and using the others' skills and experiences to strengthen their own management appropriately to meet the identified future opportunities.

In this analogy, there is no centralisation of power or authority and it works on a very straightforward distributed process. Please see also below: ***Five Precedents And Their Successes P76***

---

[21] Please see Appendix 3 – Will Schutz and FIRO-B

Often it can be better to consider strategies from outside your own market sector and modify them to your particular circumstance which can surprise the competition and delight customers.

What the Winners did was to open relationships with dissimilar organisations and swap skill-sets; for example: An advertiser sharing communication skills with an accountancy firm; the accountancy firm swapping financial control skills with the advertiser; each in an open and sharing manner.

The accountancy firm still needed to formally promote itself but could now do this more effectively and grew. The advertising company still needed to submit annual accounts and an audit, yet was much better controlled because of better financial management and new planning skills which improved profitability and reduced costs.

After a number of try-outs to establish appropriate contacts and generate the right level of trust, the Hub (identified in 2023) approached a number of selected Trade Organisations, which were closely allied with business and business people, to offer them a programme that delivered a number of Member benefits.

The programme provided an additional opportunity for their Members to link, cooperate and mutually improve their commercial operations.

The commercial improvements not only meant growth and future security for these businesses but also greater numbers of people in employment and also potentially better wages – all of which strengthened the local communities.

For the Trade Organisations this added greater involvement and support for Members, increased their Membership numbers and extended their reach into additional local business communities.

An outline of the programme

The Trade Organisations selected and contacted a number of their commercial Members, Owner-Managers and retired business people and invited them to a series of events.

The first event was designed to recognise organisations' strengths and weaknesses; not only in their current markets but also with respect to unfolding events and opportunities; the individual outputs from the first event were analysed by the Hub in strict confidence and complementary organisations identified.

Participants were invited to a second event (which they could refuse with no stigma attached).

Depending on the pairings, subsequent coaching/chaperone[22] events were held for them at appropriate time periods (usually monthly). These events were designed to best suit the participants – who would normally meet weekly at the Trade Organisation as a matter of course.

---

[22] The in Victorian times the chaperone was there to absorb the energy the two young folk created – too much energy and the relationship was likely to fly apart.

All of this was supported by the Hub which provided speakers and material for the sessions run by the Trade Organisations. The format of the sessions could be flexed, depending on the Trade Organisation or the wishes of the Members.

This is discussed in more detail below.

<u>What Characterised the Winners.</u>

The notion that the Northerner is a good fighter but a poor leader is found dotted around a number of publications and summed up by Arthur Wise in [*The day the queen ...*] "*It was something in the Northern spirit that wasn't in essence independent. It could rise like a bloody bubble of fury, but it couldn't take charge.*" Born to fight, but not born to lead – certainly something to think about.

Back in the days of management tuition we used to speak, not of leadership but of followership – what would cause you to follow this individual unhesitatingly? It seems fair that the Northerner's inherent dour nature doesn't readily reach out to others; although invention, planning and technical ability are generally taken as read.

In looking towards the winners, they were the ones that found ways to work together. As noted by Wilson & Wilson:

Selfishness beats altruism within groups. Altruistic groups beat selfish groups. Everything else is commentary.

Evolutionary biologists: Wilson & Wilson 2007.

And the challenge was to get these dour, suspicious, unadventurous characters to cooperate and actually try something that was new to them but standard for their selected business partner.

Once working together became established, the culture supported businesses that continually improved, grew and flourished, benefiting their owners and also society.

All trading businesses (to my knowledge) have to consider a number of particular and interlinked activities as simplified below:

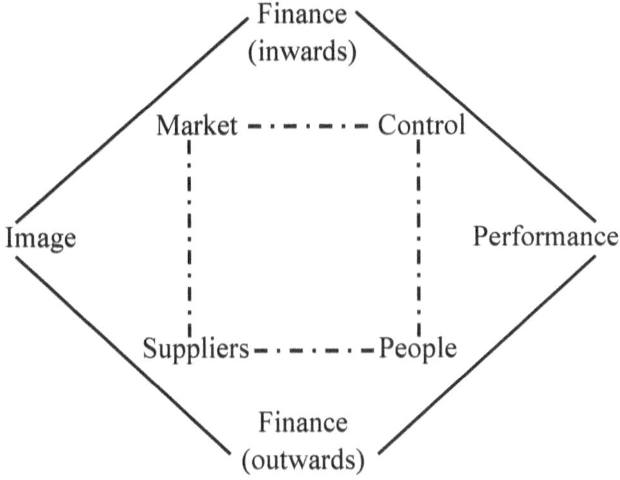

A more complete study is in
[*Beyond Money p.27 ff*].

All these elements need to be managed and coordinated; however, some organisations will rely more on one aspect than another, for example a service company will rely more on its people, and a confectionary manufacturer more on its market.

Peter Drucker[23] is generally credited with saying that *'If you can't measure it, you can't manage it'*. This simplistic notion has no doubt led to an alarming level of unnecessary paperwork and inflexible management.

That said, in the model above four of the criteria are reasonably easy to measure:

- Finance inwards – turnover.
- Finance outwards – costs.
- Performance – efficiencies in production.
- Image – Brand Share (with caution).

Brand Share needs to relate to performance in a specific market; for example it would be meaningless for a window cleaner to relate to share of windows to the UK when the market is a small part of a local town; conversely Coca Cola used to talk about gaining '2% of throat' i.e. that in their market 2% of all soft drinks would be theirs, however, not too meaningful in a pub chain, for example, with a Pepsi franchise.

Joining the more readily measurable bits are those operational considerations that can sometimes be hard to measure:

- Market – links image and income.
- Control – links income and efficiency.
- People – link efficiency and expenditure.
- Suppliers – link expenditure and image.

---

[23] Also W. Edwards Deming and Lord Kelvin

Suppliers need to be treated with a bit of caution as they include research organisations as well as service providers and suppliers of raw materials.

Having worked for high-profile brand leaders it was evident that they could negotiate better deals than some other companies because their suppliers wanted to have the reflected glory of the high-profile company to demonstrate legitimacy to their own prospective clients.

Research companies will explore, for example, image (delivered quality + perceived quality) which can lead to cost savings through value engineering.

Running alongside the model is the SWOT analysis[24] provided in some detail at **Appendix 2.**

Opportunities and Threats are in the future and external to the organisation. Strengths and Weaknesses are in the present and summarise internal management and capabilities as a prelude to selecting best-fit Opportunities.

The SWOT analysis highlights in absolute terms where an organisation needs to focus attention to best realise potential Opportunities or defuse potential Threats.

Running alongside the SWOT should be the BWOT[25] analysis which gives a wider consideration of which potential Opportunities to progress.

The BWOT analysis needs to be considered to put the organisation into its appropriate competitive

---

[24] Strengths, Weaknesses, Opportunities & Threats – the origin of the acronym is obscure.

[25] Better than, Worse than, the competition for given Opportunities and Threats

setting. BWOT considers the same factors, but from a different perspective.

With two co-operating organisations sharing experience and information, this analysis will also help to inform the complementary organisation, that is the selected commercial partner, where sharing intelligence is not only efficient but also cost-saving.

How The Winners Achieved Success.

Here, I use the analogy of a boat (stock market) where the captain (investment banks) can't be blamed for it slowly sinking into the quagmire of half promises, obfuscation and patronage, with the crew (the politicians) flittering from life-boat to life-boat without ever quite reaching the shore – but measuring and documenting every step assiduously.

Meantime, the successful passengers (smaller businesses) have banded together in cohesive groups, each with a prominent leader and complementary strengths, reached the shore and set up camp. They still have to revisit the stricken hulk from time to time because of belongings they have left there. The real winners on the shore have set up trading posts, playing to their different collective strengths: hunting, farming, building and making things.

They have also got to work more closely with the local people, not only supplying, and being supplied by, these local people but also supporting one another.

This ability to work in an agile manner, as altruistic groups under sound leadership, developed a number of win-win relationships where the camps on the shore provided goods and services valued by the local people and the local people trading food and supplies for these goods and services – although not necessarily in the currency the winners had brought ashore or left on the boat.

A Model for Success.

In analysing the shipwreck; the winning settlers on the shore exhibited five key traits:

- Complementary organisations swapping know-how, suppliers and opportunities.
- Organisations integrating to mutually optimise productivity, assets and distribution.
- Financial support, provided mutually, without demands for immediate returns.
- External specialist support, provided as needed.
- Available and reliable tradespeople when new opportunities presented themselves.

<u>The Two-Pronged Attack.</u>

A number of different types of small and medium-sized enterprises (SMEs) can be characterised, not just from markets they operate in and the goods and services they provide, but also by how they are structured and managed.

To keep some sort of order, out of the myriad types of SME, I am using just two types of organisation to book-end the SMEs that got together for mutual benefit and for the benefit of society.

These extremes may be characterised on the one hand as the owner/manager and, on the other hand, the mature family business.

<u>The Owner/Manager.</u>

Organisations that may be represented here generally focus on one, or just a few, goods or services and can include the corner shop as well as the local garage or plumber; some working from their own premises, some working from home and some visiting premises in which to work. These organisations may employ staff, such as the carpet seller/fitter or work alone like the window-cleaner.

Generally, the owner/managers work for themselves and the organisation prospers or falls almost exclusively on the strength of their commitment, involvement and enthusiasm.

There is usually a desire to grow but an uncertainty about how to go about growth and a reluctance to commit to hiring staff – chicken and egg when it comes to balancing extra staff costs with potential increased revenue from expansion.

A number of businesses started because of a good idea or a gap in the local market; many realised their potential when an outsider pointed out their fundamental market and the real benefits the trader delivered.

By drawing together dissimilar but complementary organisations each learned from the other (even sharing the cost of an administrator for example) and put the foundations in place to support expansion and, with that expansion, the opportunity to employ a greater number of people and benefit local society whilst both organisations grew and flourished.

The Mature Family Business.

These organisations have often got to the fourth generation[26] or beyond; and many such organisations are still in the tight grip of the family.

For some, there is no great desire to get significantly bigger, build more branch outlets or become franchisors; there is often, however, a strong

---

[26] Old rule of thumb: first generation starts it, second generation grows it, third generation trashes it and the fourth generation rescues it.

and meaningful relationship with their local community – whether through the Church, social organisations, civic rôles or more formal gathering such as Rotary or the Free Masons.

In bringing organisations such as this together and their being big enough to foster innovation, confident enough to invest and ambitious enough to train[27], efficiencies were improved and net profit increased to the point where there was an appetite to further support the local communities – communities that had been abandoned by central government and all but neglected by local government as services had been cut to the bone.

In their way, each type of business supported their local communities: by hiring more people, investing in their activities or by direct intervention in community welfare.

All of which enriched the County.

The Process.

The Trade Organisations that brought the various companies together had a good understanding of the differences between the various types of organisation and their Members so were readily able to balance the complementary strengths of those participating.

---

[27] A bit like Germany's Mittelstand

<u>The Mating Game.</u>

Events were organised by a Hub through Trade Organisations for their Members to create stronger commercial linkages, encourage the sharing of commercial nous and give each Member a 'reference point' in another organisation where they could go for free, relevant and practical advice.

Such Organisations included for example: Rotary Clubs, Chambers of Commerce, Accountancy firms, the Chartered Management Institute and the Federation of Small Businesses.

<u>Note</u>: The drive is to link commercial organisations; a number of Member organisations are active in the political arena and these should be sidelined for now; their turn will come later.

One of the benefits from using Trade Organisations is that there was already a good bond between the various Members of that Organisation and a degree of mutual respect between those Members that could be developed further.

The Trade Organisations contacted their commercial Members, Owner-Managers and retired business people and invited them to a series of events.

The first event was designed to recognise organisations' strengths and weaknesses; not only in their current markets but also with respect to unfolding events and opportunities.

The individual outputs from the first event were passed to the Hub in strict confidence for analysis. The analyses and complementary organisations were identified to the particular Trade Organisation.

Members were supplied with a copy of their own analysis and the name (but no more) of their complementary organisation. After time to ponder the output of their analysis and who the complementary organisation was, Members were invited to a second event (which they could refuse with no stigma attached).

<u>Event Structure.</u>

Those participants enthusiastic to meet came together at a second event, were paired up and invited to compare analyses and how they might support one another.

Depending on the pairings, subsequent coaching/chaperone events were held for them at appropriate time periods (usually monthly). These events were designed to best suit the participants – who would normally meet weekly at the Trade Organisation as a matter of course.

All of this was supported by the Hub which provided speakers and material for the sessions run by the Trade Organisations. The format of the sessions could be flexed, depending on the Trade Organisation or the wishes of the Members.

The first session followed the basic format of:

- Welcome, set the scene, outline the session and provide each delegate with two short questionnaires to complete – one to keep for reference and reflection, the other to submit for analysis if they felt this would be right for them. Questionnaires to be completed when instructed.
- A formal presentation of the key elements of business with some basic considerations including: brand strength, financial ratios, objectivity and negotiation; the aim being to cause delegates to step back a little from their day-to-day issues and become more objective about how their own organisation is managed.
- Delegates then completed a *Today* section of the questionnaire – current Strengths & Weaknesses.
- A second presentation explored the external environment, what is happening and how this may impact on the future success of an organisation; in particular changes, trends and catastrophes in: technology, climate, availability of finance and political activity.
- Delegates then complete an *Ideal* section of the questionnaire – how well prepared might they be for the future.
- There then followed an open forum and general discussion when delegates could make any changes to the questionnaires, given time to reflect and any additional information.

- Delegates retained a copy of their questionnaire, the second copy was provided for analysis if the delegate wished to move to the next stage.
- Contact details exchanged, thanks and finish.

Following the event the questionnaires were analysed by the Hub, looking in particular for two attributes:

- The gaps between *Today* and *Ideal* for each criterion – to highlight where organisations might benefit from additional support.
- To identify the high scores for categories in *Ideal* – to identify organisations which can potentially give that support.

Trade Organisations were then contacted, the paired Members were identified and invited to get together at a second event, recognising that some organisations were receiving as well as giving.

Second sessions were then organised, the content of which was based on the Members attending and their particular analysed needs. These needs advised the specialist supporters/coaches of the business areas to consider in more depth which would then be formally considered.

After each presentation the paired Members were invited to withdraw up and interrogate one other to drill down deeper, clarify objectives and better look to each other's future and how each could help the other without compromising commercial confidentiality.

Typical areas of specialist support included:

- The purpose of the organisation being to deliver benefits (profits come from doing this well).
- What benefits (tangible & intangible) each organisation delivers.
- What differentiates each organisation in the market place (falling from this came how organisations can complement one another when clearer about their different customers).
- Setting meaningful objectives and how this relates to staff development.

Other topics were included as considered appropriate to the cross section of Members. Paired delegates then set appropriate learning/development activities for each other and, subsequently, the Hub provided specialist support if necessary, but was rarely used.

Further events were organised with respect to the organisations' particular needs, time constraints and business considerations, supported by the Hub which managed the database and reminders to meet. The Hub also monitored results, quality of delivery and 'training the trainers'.

<u>A Result.</u>

The majority of the contributing organisations flourished, grew, improved profitability, invested back in the business, employed more people and paid better wages than their competitors which gave a wider selection of talented people (including some from the declining public sector and big companies). A positive feed-back loop that could be constantly refined, developed and publicised.

The modern (2027) 'mill owners' began to invest in education, culture and society because they could see even greater returns for themselves than they would get by investing in land, property or even the stock market.

Education led to more talented staff, cultural intervention provided better mental health and the 'mill owners' influence in society grew through their having greater time to devote to working as local mayors or counsellors.

<u>Five Precedents And Their Successes:</u>

This success was not a new phenomenon; as a business consultant I've applied this approach on numerous occasions with some clients growing at 20% per annum compound for several years.

The approach has also been evidenced in Trade Organisations and Membership Bodies; some examples are detailed below.

<u>Informal Gatherings.</u>

<u>Precedent 1</u>. It is not unusual for accountancy firms, legal firms and other professional advisors to invite clients to meet together informally over drinks from time to time. These gatherings not only allow the professional bodies to update their clients but also clients to share concerns and provide informal support to one another outside these gatherings.

Success. At one such meeting an MD of a small organisation was chatting with his accountant; who I knew; and was referred to me – his requirements were not my strength but an associate had the necessary skills and significantly improved the small business.

<u>A Chamber of Commerce.</u>

<u>Precedent 2</u>. Several of us were heavily involved with the Chamber and would run one-day workshops for its Members; workshops such as financial planning, personnel management, marketing, negotiating etc.

Almost regardless of the topic under discussion, the day would start with a degree of tension between delegates where each saw the other as competitive. By early afternoon just about everyone was cooperating – most had realised that as a SME there was no way they could serve the whole of a major London borough.

However, the delegates did begin to refer leads and suppliers between themselves which led to stronger growth, and increased future security.

Success. Anecdotal evidence from subsequent chamber meetings confirmed the organisations that had easily and naturally got to work together showed growth and greater efficiency.

In time, this cooperation would begin to fade as more immediate issues took over; however, refresher days worked well and brought people back together and re-establish the mutual benefits.

<u>Bringing large and small together.</u>

<u>Precedent </u>3. A different style of event was managed for a Major London Organisation (MLO) which was claiming to be supporting local SMEs but the local SMEs were unconvinced; all that had happened was a plethora of reports, written to flatter the directors of MLO – reports that were duly shelved whilst life carried on as normal.

We brought together: two Directors of the MLO, twelve buyers/negotiators and 50-odd local SMEs. The subsequent impact of actually discussing the MLO's needs and opportunities with a range of (exasperated?) sidelined SMEs had a much more significant impact than the usual bland report in that a good degree of emotion was involved.

About fifteen opportunities were recognised and also the means to achieve them were identified.

<u>**Success.**</u> The results of this particular exercise were that:

- five out of sixteen procurement requirements were amended to make doing business easier – things such as allowing collective insurance rather than each supplier having to have at least £10m of insurance – even if only a sandwich van supplying an outside workforce.
- Seven of the participating companies gained new meaningful work.

Other benefits included:

- Not having to have less than 25% of your annual turnover as the value of the contract.
- Some policies were considered unnecessary such as ageism and were waived.
- It wasn't necessary to have had a 10-year track record of profitability or a balance sheet above a particular value.

Later conversations with the directors of the MLO, and subsequently confirmed by a number of the small businesses, recognised that several of the recommendations had actually been implemented and some of the rules amended.

The exercise benefited the local commercial community and kept opportunities within the area – opportunities that had for too long been realised from outside the borough; and, additionally, benefited the MLO by increasing the range, variety and price-points of (now) eligible suppliers

<u>Peter Doyle, Warwick University.</u>

<u>Precedent</u> 4. Back in the 1980s (personal report now lost, so from memory) there was interest in how Japanese car manufacturing plants in the UK were noticeably more productive than British car manufacturers in the UK

Both sets of operations being managed almost exclusively by British people who had been, British educated and the plants subject to the same costs of services and availability of parts.

Peter Doyle ran a series of comparisons into cooperation between manufacturers and suppliers in Japan, in the UK and in America. It turned out that the Japanese manufacturers in Japan were the most cost-effective and productive, UK were good and America poor.

It turned out that in Japan there is a high degree of trust between organisations where their level of cooperation went as far as sending top engineers to supplier plants to improve efficiencies and reduce costs; suppliers were brought into the car manufacturers to see how things were done and encouraged to modify production where there might be an advantage – a very open and trusting relationship.

In the UK there was good arms-length relationships between manufacturer and supplier but each was a little wary of the other and would not open up as much as in Japan.

The Americans played at it, looking to see what could be taken for their own advantage and readily changing suppliers if they thought there was a bit of an advantage to be had.

The key determinant (from memory) was the level of trust and openness which not only improved productivity but also created long-lasting relationships because of the mutual benefits that accrued.

Success. When with the Business Link I applied the same logic to a number of companies and gradually opened more substantial relationships with their suppliers.

In time, the suppliers worked on the factory floor to better understand the changes required and (equally importantly) how to implement them.

Taking two of the companies as examples, one company tripled its annual profit; the other reduced the working week and the MD got to play golf on a Saturday – something long denied because of business demands.

Management Research Groups.

Precedent 5. Established by the Chartered Management Institute, these Groups met one a month over eight months a year (missing winter) for dinner in private for an off-the-record discussion.

The invited attendees were CEOs, Major Company Directors and Managing Partners, plus a guest provided by the Institute.

The invited guest was recommended by the Institute and often a senior member of an organisation that had run into a brick wall with some sort of management problem.

The guest stated the situation and why it was problematic (e.g. unsure how to diversify, or realise an opportunity); questions and answers to clarify exactly what was needed and then experience, expertise and knowledge would be shared.

Success. For example, one guest was three years into a five-year major reorganisation and centralisation of a disparate organisation comprising tens of outlying centres and several thousand staff.

One of the regular attendees was CEO of a major (highly respected) multi-national who had faced a very similar situation, other Members had also had similar experiences, but not at the same level.

The dinner ended with a solution that had already been shown to work and was subsequently implemented.

<u>The Role of Culture</u>

Yorkshire and the broader North has long been recognised as a centre for cultural innovation as well as technical and technological development.

Historically, art and culture developed in the North has been managed, in the main, by London companies[28] who had the distribution, contacts and muscle to profit from others' material.

Here is a major opportunity to link culture, technology and production to get people back to the music hall or the pub (where it seems a lot of good ideas are generated through interaction) with devices like those old pub tabletops where, for a shilling, you could play space invaders, pac-man or tennis. Instead you now rent ear-buds from the bar, invoke virtual reality and watch a play, a football match or a concert on a piece of kit too expensive for the home and big enough to dwarf the 72" TV.

Here are opportunities for creatives to link with technologists to create apps, or similar, distributed on-line with their management, promotion and control held in Yorkshire and the profit spent here in the County, not siphoned off to London or to the aggressively mediocre[29] 'Middle England'.

And, many good uprisings start with a good song.

---

[28] There were a few exceptions such as Factory Records, but these were few and far between.
[29] A favourite oxymoron – fighting to maintain the status quo.

A number of organisations are working towards co-ordinating businesses to give the benefits of synergy, but working to different models.

Three groupings that spring readily to mind are noted below but with their specific details removed.

- An on-line group that extends throughout and beyond Yorkshire which is great for swapping data and information but to make a difference there needs to be a deeper relationship that can swap and share knowledge, experience and understanding. I've tried it and it is nowhere as productive as a relaxed conversation over a beer.

- A political conglomeration that has spent the last five years discussing what might be done and addressing minor organisations but with little or no progress and no promise of progress.

- A political party that favours the economists' clusters, tending towards the more substantial city-located businesses and not developing the benefit of inputs from dissimilar organisations.

Progress Report.

2023.

After a tentative start a few Membership Organisations agreed to 'give it a try' – flying in the face of Yorkshire stubbornness and the "if it were right for me dad, it's right enough for me" attitude.

Initial results were patchy – a bit like marriages that have lasted beyond 25 years: One third of Cooperatives *lived happily together*, one third *were together for convenience* and one third *divorced*.

By the end of the year there were a few very positive results, but enough to provide the energy to continue.

AROUND THIS TIME, BIG COMPANIES WERE EXPERIENCING A REDUCTION IN SALES BUT AN INCREASE IN CLAMOUR FROM SHAREHOLDERS FOR DIVIDEND, WHICH CAUSED THEM TO TAKE THEIR EYES OFF THEIR MARKETS.

Natural resources.

The impact of the Russia/Ukraine war opened access to deposits of manganese, lithium, uranium, graphite and some rare earths which were made more readily available. To help pay for the war incoming traders started new businesses and industry and academia began to develop new and useful applications.

<u>**2024.**</u>

ELECTION YEAR, CENTRAL GOVERNMENT WAS PROPPING UP THE BIG COMPANIES TO SHOW FULL EMPLOYMENT, PRETENDING THEY CARED AND LAYING THE GROUNDWORK TO BE RE-ELECTED. SMALL COMPANIES WERE SIDELINED.

In order to refine the process. The Hub undertook an exercise to study the various types of Cooperative identified in 2023.

One of the key findings was that the declared objectives from the various *Together for Convenience* Cooperatives were neither clear not market-focused, some objectives had drifted without the knowledge of the other party.

On looking more closely at the *Happily Together* Cooperatives it became clear that one of the very positive traits exhibited by them was that they were absolutely clear in their purpose, each continually refining the defined benefits and not only looking out for their own opportunities and threats but bringing intelligence to their partners; they also had the fortitude and resilience to actually challenge one another robustly but positively[30].

Those that had *divorced* had gone back to their old ways.

---

[30] For the development of mutually beneficial relationships please see **Appendix 3 Will Schutz and FIRO-B.**

The findings were shared between the Trade Organisations to circulate amongst their Members. This action, re-forged some relationships, strengthened others and increased Members' success rates quite measurably.

The Trade Organisations were also beginning to talk to one another informally, more freely and with greater purpose.

Prior to the election, national unemployment had fallen. That was about to change.

<u>**2025.**</u>

ELECTION OVER – THE WINNING PARTY SPENT MUCH OF THE YEAR GETTING TO GRIPS WITH THE SHAMBLES IT HAD TO MANAGE, CONTINUING TO SUPPORT BIG COMPANIES[31] AND IGNORING THE VARIOUS SMEs.

However, those elected and moving into power (Prime Minister and Ministers) all tended to be from the legal profession (unlike in physics; with people, like tends to attract like) and this took us back to the late 1980s when we had moved from innovation through implementation and were entering a period of imposition.

---

[31] To the tune of a chunk of £20bn and using the age-old tactic of *Research Grants* where only the big firms had departments set up to deal with government bureaucracy; the 'grants' were, in effect, simply a tax-offset to keep those companies in the UK.

This year was the start of those 'important' and 'difficult decisions' delivering 'what the people really want' that is 'affordable and reasonable'.

'Going forward' politicians now had three & a half years before they had to account for their actions.

The big firms were losing sight of their markets and shedding staff in an effort to continue to pay shareholders their expected ever-increasing dividends, which gave rise to a couple of unexpected benefits for the small firms:

- New market opportunities were emerging for the smaller firms, for example micro-breweries.
- The 'redundant' staff – many of whom were very skilled – were looking for work.

Meantime, the Trade Organisations and Cooperative Members were consolidating, developing constructive ways of working better together and beginning to reach out into their communities with local meetings and events, more or less unnoticed by a government that had its own problems.

2026.

The number of 'Hub co-ordinated' Trade Organisations is steadily growing spreading out from the cities into the towns and even parts of the countryside.

The Hub established a small marketing group to recruit new Trade Organisations and to support those where an expert speaker might be required to facilitate the of the various Members cooperating.

Additionally, sharing widely best commercial practice and recognising more specifically what is right for the County, its industry and its people.

Despite all the positive activity, this cooperation programme was still, in effect, a cottage industry and the government wasn't helping by maintaining the plethora of regulations and mountain of bureaucracy demanded by the detail-obsessed lawyers who still didn't understand business, despite their claims to be 'on top of things'[32] – those individuals who were voted in as Members Of Parliament in 2024.

It is this level of regulation and compliance that needed to be broken down to make any real progress.

Despite little change in how Westminster governs, the Cooperative Yorkshire organisations continued to flourish and others were beginning to notice.

---

[32] Oh, you know all the words, and you sung all the notes
But you never quite learned the song, she sang
I can tell by the sadness in your eyes
That you never quite learned the song.
The Hedgehog Song, Incredible String Band 1967

2027 A Summary of Benefits.

<u>Businesses.</u>
One benefit of working through Trade Organisations is that people meet and mingle from all types of businesses whether owner/managed or locally long established. Co-operation is the order of the day is continuing to further new relationships.

This approach opens new opportunities and additional benefits for the <u>owner/managed</u> businesses which include:

- Working together, the owner/managed firms improved their marketing, increased their efficiencies and generated greater profits to invest in their businesses, and were more prepared to take on (or share) extra staff and train people.
- Additional opportunities to provide goods and services to established local family firms through closer association and increased trust.
- Advice on upcoming opportunities was shared as the local family firms opened new business and exploited new developments.
- Opportunities for funding became available where the local family firms could lend money without the strictures of a bank and could take equity in a small company (or a development by a small company).

For the <u>established local family firms</u> (a bit like the German Mittelstand), some of the benefits that they derived from co-operation were:

- Business support from specialist members of the Hub and also the smaller organisations – many of which can provide specialist or informal advice.
- Smaller organisations developing new ideas into products and processes that can be deployed directly into the larger organisation.
- A testing-ground for new products through informal 'assessment in use' by the smaller organisations.
- Increased profitability through better targeted sales, more efficient admin and tighter controls where they had adopted some of the smaller organisations' ways of working.
- Access to very skilled people leaving the public sector, either through desire or redundancy, most needed some re-orientation to a profit-driven environment but those that adapted proved to be very useful and skilful staff.

For Larger Organisations.

It has not just been the SME sector that has benefited; bigger organisations have also gained the advantage of more agile suppliers and there is also major investment where there is a willingness to adapt, supported by deep-water ports.

Heavy engineering has roots in Hull, Tyneside and Sheffield where the more astute people have recognised the need for strategic infrastructure and associated products made in the UK, avoiding dependency on unreliable imports; such products as railway lines, aircraft components, sources of renewable energy (e.g. windfarms). All have benefited from a capable workforce and appropriate sites to build or to re-establish factories.

One world-class example is Forgemasters which manufactures strategically important things and has a significant emphasis on research and development. This culture of excellence can be translated to other critical industries with ideas and experiences shared cooperatively.

The UK has always had a dependency on imported food, made worse by Brexit and despite any agreements with other countries or trading blocs. Coupled with climate change, this opened opportunities for the development of agricultural products not native to the UK and also for food processing plants.

<u>Society.</u>

The various commercial activities and their cooperative development is benefiting society in a number of ways:
- The smaller companies, in growing, employ more local people and contribute to the increasing wealth of the area.

- Complementary businesses are working together to foster greater local self-sufficiency which is becoming increasingly important because infrastructure is still erratic and unreliable.
- The bigger family companies are now getting deeper into local politics to ensure support goes to the most appropriate causes – not only food banks and charities but also the arts which enriches the lives of local people.
- All organisations are growing, becoming more technical, and employing more workers – all of which improves peoples' lot across the County.

Meanwhile elsewhere in the UK.

This is a time of worry for Westminster where overseas banks (and UK banks) have recognised, and finally acknowledged, the weak financial management by UK politicians; Money Market Traders are moving from London's Square Mile and away from the weakening Pound Sterling to Frankfurt and Paris with the stronger €Euro, as are the banks' head offices.

Not only is there worry over the banks and currency, but the surplus staff taken on prior to the election (to demonstrate full employment) and who expected jobs for life are now seen as a drain and are being laid off, releasing some very capable people who are now looking for work.

The totality of the UK economy is failing despite tighter regulation and yet more of it. This is looking increasingly like a year of transition when the privileged wealthy are seeing their net worth declining and their investments aren't earning enough. A number of these people are talking about shedding their peerages and standing for the next election in order to protect their estates.

By now a number of companies have banded together cooperated and risen above the chaos and awful management, that characterises central government, to become more self-sufficient – even trading with European companies.

The model that Yorkshire developed is being orchestrated through business, not through politics and, whilst locally implemented, is readily scalable and spread easily across the whole of Yorkshire – and beyond.

Such is the success with the associated independence that other regions are beginning to follow; and, there is the possibility that the North as a whole might unite[33] to bring back a quality of life, and the dignity so long denied, to 16 million people by the inward-looking London-centric governance the country has lived with for so many years.

---

[33] Northumberland, for example could have been pretty isolated – trapped between Yorkshire and Scotland.

Part 3. Looking Forward from 2027

In anticipating the dynamics as we emerge into 2028 it seems we might be on the threshold of invention and divergence, overseen by a new style of hands-off legislator who is progressive in their thinking, reluctant to interfere and prepared to invest in people, expansion and technology.

In Northern Ireland Sinn Fein had become the dominant party in the 2025 election and also dominant in the Republic of Ireland about the same time. there was a focus on Ireland re-unifying.

Scotland became more resolute in suing for independence and Wales distanced itself from Westminster.

These were significant developments that occupied a great deal of Westminster's time – in effect, a diversion that supported people setting up informal local groups, all working with purpose and below the government 'radar', avoiding political interference and having the time to become properly established.

In addition, the changes of government in the UK and also in Europe opened the way for on-going win-win negotiations (instigated by Brussels!) instead of the ludicrous win-lose negotiations which had been the tone since Brexit

THE BIG FIRMS ARE STRUGGLING, POLITICIANS ARE LOSING IMAGINARY POWER, WESTMINSTER IS A LAUGHING-STOCK AND YORKSHIRE IS INCREASING IN CONFIDENCE.

The influence of the Hub has grown significantly, supported by the Trade Organisations to the point that they actually have a voice.

All of which opened the way to increase growth in Yorkshire business and enhance support for our local communities.

By banding together, and working <u>through</u> Trade Organisations, appointments and influence have been generated for SMEs that they wouldn't have achieved on their own.

<u>Beyond 2027</u>

<u>2029 Onwards & Upwards.</u>

My first book is a study of the feasibility of Yorkshire as an independent state (the destination); this second book is the first step on that journey and opens a process for SMEs to work better together in order to create not only better business practices but also commercial opportunities with major organisations and government departments – big entities where less than 11% of contracts are awarded to UK SMEs (despite what they boast).

This disparity needed to be addressed and it is anticipated that now the Yorkshire SMEs are working properly together they will provide a strong enough force to influence the governance of the County for the benefit of all of its people.

The goals of 2029 and forward are:

- To continue to develop and strengthen the co-operation between Trade Organisations.
- To encourage established family businesses to get more involved in their local societies.
- To continue to develop the Hub to provide increasingly relevant and sophisticated support to the Trade Organisations.
- To maintain face-to-face links and events with the big firms and government suppliers to drive for more local business.

However, back in Westminster. Labour, now elected, have not been realising their promised potential (being driven by legally trained Ministers) and a number of the more adventurous labour peers have been dismayed by the increasing regulation and rigidity which is continuing to drive investment overseas.

Despite being in their sixties and seventies, seeing their wealth ebbing away, these peers have thrown off their ermine & tassels to stand at the 2029 election – unsurprisingly in safe seats – and got stuck in.

These are individuals who have significant traction in the financial world and were determined that their personal wealth and status should be maintained (rescuing the fiat money) and despite many being in their 60s and 70s they still have the energy that Churchill (77), Macmillan (63) and Douglas Home (60) had when they were appointed Prime Minister.

Some of their activities included:

- Increasing Central Government efficiency.
- Reducing the size of the public sector.
- Devolving (non-financial & investment) decisions to the regions.
- Minimising additional bureaucracy.

With attention now being diverted to fiat money, a new initiative is in preparation to take a more realistic approach to economics and societal money.

An initiative that recognised how societal economics and distributed politics can work better together for benefit to commerce and communities and not just Westminster and the bankers.

This involved:

- An economic model and advice for the politicians that makes practical sense, can be readily understood, delivers genuine benefits to society and brings the movement of all types money back under control.
- A meaningful initiative to engage the political circles and raise the profile and capabilities of Yorkshire within Westminster to get the investment necessary for the County to flourish and realise its true potential.
- The establishment of a *County Quorum*[34] that supports and guides the Hub, coordinating local Member Organisations and begins to open the way to greater independence.

---

[34] Please see [*Yorkshire, The Case For Independence*] Pg 22 ff.

- Having developed a system that works, the Quorum will begin to lobby and engage politicians to reform the rules relating to investment, insurance and pensions amongst the larger established investors; private investment will also be encouraged to provide a healthy degree of competition.
- Normally, about 50% of productivity increases are due to innovation and invention, these rule changes will allow funds to be released for new and exciting projects – not all with success 100% guaranteed but with a high probability of net profit for the investor.
- A number of centres will be established to help companies 'work smarter not harder'; these will engage the universities who are already involved with companies in original research and 'persistent experimentation' to develop new opportunities and new materials with potential for future applications.
- Training will be provided that runs alongside product and idea development to balance practical understanding with the application of theory.

Historically, government has never been tasked with making a profit[35]. It's very easy to spend someone else's money and if you run out, raise taxes or ride on quantitative easing.

---

[35] So has continued with out-dated inadequate systems that maintain the impression of power and retain the status quo.

The next step on the journey is to look back from 2036 and explore how closer coordinated relationships between commerce, academia, society and government led to a more balanced, productive and coordinated Yorkshire.

Yorkshire – now sitting on top of England.

A new wave of politicians are coming (slowly) to the fore developing the *County Quorum,* noted above; this includes peers prepared to 'let go' and allow development to happen whilst replacing the small coterie of Westminster elites who were beginning to look increasingly irrelevant.

The door was beginning to open to society-focused economists who were replacing the traditional rhetoric and wrong assumptions noted earlier and were beginning to be listened to by the politicians who were increasingly supporting the people they represented, not a political party, banking or an elite clique which had wielded imaginary power and mis-directed influence for so long.

This involvement with selected politicians and differently focused economics will be the subject of the next step on this journey.[36]

---

[36] Provisionally planned for release in 2024

Appendices

Appendix 1. Ponzi and Inflation.

Whole books have been written on this topic; one that is worth a read is [*Planet Ponzi*] which describes a scheme set up early in the 1900s when Charles Ponzi landed in Boston and after a few experiments set up an investment scheme that was too good to be true.

The scheme worked by paying the investors their dividends from new registrations, so as long as the scheme grew there was increasing income to pay increasing dividends to increasing numbers of investors – with Charles Ponzi taking a percentage of all the money 'invested'.

So far so good – except recruitment and joining fees are linear and pay-out is based on incremental growth, so at some time, by definition, the net position must go negative – as shown in the graph below.

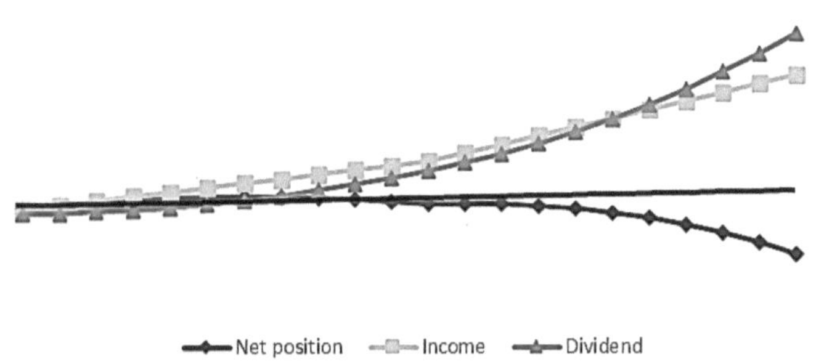

Such a scheme must inevitably run out of new punters, collapse and leave a whole bunch of people destitute whilst the originator of the scheme slides happily into the sunset, many millions of pounds better off.

Let's now turn to central government and imagine the waves of 'quantitative easing' as hopeful punters expecting a return on their investment – in this instance paid from a number of sources including taxation and, importantly, paid from the next wave of quantitative easing and kept affordable through inflation reducing the real value of the original bond issues that set the ball rolling in the first place.

As a country, we have continual borrowing through government bonds (income) to fund exponentially increasing expenditure (dividend) on unemployment, inflation, wages, pensions, care, neglected infrastructure, health, education etc. etc. plus interest and capital repayments.

This bubble has to burst but meanwhile, it keeps the investment bankers in gin & tonic whilst maintaining a small clique of elite politicians and their privileged chums in misplaced power, and the rest of the country in poverty.

What has grown up is a coterie of Politicians neglecting all but the City of London, Westminster, themselves and their favoured cronies. It's a massive fraud and the bubble must eventually burst.

Unfortunately, Yorkshire doesn't fit any of the above categories and so we must find a way to look out for ourselves – through cooperation.

<u>Appendix 2 – SWOT Deconstructed.</u>

<u>*Making Best Use of SWOT.*</u>

SWOT – Strengths, Weaknesses, Opportunities and Threats – compartmentalising the things that can help drive business or can cause significant problems.

The SWOT can still provide a very useful and simple mechanism to bring organisations and groups together provided it is used well, it gives the users a broad view of external affairs and a critical view of internal management.

This is an acronym that would be better placed as OTSW because the OT (Opportunities & Threats) lie outside the organisation and, generally, into the future.

The SW (Strengths & Weaknesses) are internal and relative to market and competition. Addressing them should be considered by the organisation as it is managed today and in relation to how it intends to take advantage of the future Opportunities and Threats.

<u>*Opportunities and Threats.*</u>

The Opportunities & Threats are external to the organisation and in the future – things happening elsewhere that can have a knock-on effect.

An effect that can give rise to unexpected opportunities (big profits from supplying energy) or, in the extreme, can close the organisation (banning a particular compound).

Please note the Opportunities are external events and not to be confused with business Options which are alternative management approaches (and internal to the business).

Another acronym (sorry!) that can be used to list the various Opportunities and Threats is PEST or its extended version PESTELL.

PESTELL[37] Analysis – a useful acronym.

The headings below should be considered in the light of: local, regional, national and international influence. The SME can be influenced as much by Brussels as by the local council re-classifying the road.

A number of specifics have already been considered to give context to the events leading up to 2027; this is simply a list to act as a memory-jerker when considering a business strategy for example:

---

[37] Believed to be developed from ETPS by Francis J Aguilar, changed to PEST, then expanded to PESTELL and beyond.

Politics:
a) International – embargos, withdrawal of agricultural grants.
b) National – housing requirements, change of party.
c) Local – parking restrictions.
d) Customer – reduce dependency on suppliers.

Economics:
a) Monopoly power e.g. OPEC.
b) Exchange rates.
c) Interest rates.
d) Global shortage of key resources.

Sociology [and demographics]:
a) Ageing population.
b) Changing spending patterns.
c) Declining skills base.
d) Migration, emigration, immigration.

Technology:
a) Alternative solutions.
b) Fast obsolescence [Lotus, Word Perfect]
c) Increasing dependency on technology.
d) Data security

Environment:
a) Packaging.
b) Emissions.
c) Discharges.
d) Remove, replace, re-use.

Legislation – staying up with changes:
   a) Individual – ageism, sexism.
   b) Organisation – statutory rights.
   c) Society – minimum wage.
   d) Imbalance in access to justice

Litigation:
   a) Equality, Intellectual Property, Data
      Protection.
   b) Awareness at all levels.
   c) Ambulance chasing lawyers.
   d) Cost of a protracted case.

The following sources of Opportunities and Threats can also be considered:

Weather – Climate change, holidays, ice cream, migration, relocation and flood barriers.

Culture – Serving across boundaries; managing, or getting, a workforce to operate differently.

Religion – Can impact on something as basic as time off or obligatory holidays. Can open opportunities as well as closing off opportunities.

Epidemics – Bird Flu closing boundaries or preventing trade; not only Covid or Monkey Pox. Epidemics can have a major impact on politics, especially in the USA.

War or Terrorism – Increased security and embargos, technology, currency, food, water, supply chains (piracy?). Not always guns and bombs.

Appendix 3. – Will Schutz and FIRO-B.

Schutz did a great deal of good work with the US navy during the 1950s; working in submarines under the Arctic for months at a time, researching what it is that fosters people to work together effectively and well.

Simply and very briefly put, he identified three phases in relationships:

- **A Common Objective.**

    Agreed by all (delivery of a defined benefit) which leads to:

- **Authority <u>with</u> Responsibility.**

    For example, the finance director has a lot of authority but not much responsibility; the sales director has a lot of responsibility but not much authority. Having a common objective brings these together which leads to:

- **Openness.**

    People can speak freely without the other party taking umbrage or becoming swollen-chested, issues are resolved easily, loss of face is not an issue, everybody learns and the organisation makes genuine progress.

As an aside, relationships come apart in reverse order, free speech is challenged, decisions queried and people migrate to different business options (grow, consolidate, diversify etc. etc.).

Disclaimer.

I have endeavoured to ensure information is current, accurate and appropriate; however, things change and priorities get reassigned.

I cannot warrant or represent the completeness, accuracy or fitness for purpose of the material provided here when used by a third party – you will have to conduct your own research, as you see appropriate, and reach your own conclusions.

This book is not a substitute for professional advice and the author will not be held liable for any damages, losses or consequential losses arising from using the material in this publication for any purpose whatsoever.

Over the course of fifty or so years I have attended lectures, joined groups, taken memberships and argued with lots of people – many of whom sparked some of the ideas and conclusions presented here. I have not kept meticulous notes and if I have failed to acknowledge anyone please get in touch and I will rectify the matter in the next edition.

The thought, approaches and calculations are mine alone and I take full responsibility for any inaccuracies or mis-representations and will take whatever corrective action is required in the next edition.

Bibliography.

Note:

The books below have informed more than just one single point; for that reason I have provided only the author, title and ISBN to avoid an unnecessary long and detailed bibliography.

Books Mentioned in the Text:

- Abhijit Banerjee & Esther Duflo. *Good Economics for Hard Times*. ISBN 978-0-241-30689-5.
- Alan Duncan. *In The Thick of It*. ISBN 978-0-00-842226-4.
- Mitch Feierstein. *Planet Ponzi*. ISBN 978-0-552-77827-5.
- Philip Goodchild. *Theology of Money*. ISBN 978-0-334-04142-9.
- Jodie Jackson. *You Are What You Read*. ISBN 978-1-78325-722-9.
- Steve Keen. *Can we Avoid Another Financial Crisis?* ISBN 978-1-509-51373-4.
- Benoit Mandelbrot. *The (Mis)behaviour of Markets*. ISBN 978-1-84668-262-9.
- Steve Mullins. *Beyond Money*. ISBN 978-1-789-55829-6.
- Steve Mullins. *Yorkshire - The Case For Independence*. ISBN 978-1-800-31899-1.

- Joe Navarro. *Dangerous Personalities.* ISBN 978-1-635-65336-6.
- Malcolm Prowle (Ed). *Reforming Public Policy Through Elected Regional Government.* ISBN 978-1-032-06356-0.
- Sheldon Rampton & John Stauber. *Trust us We're Experts.* ISBN 978-1-585-42139-8.
- James Rickards. *Currency Wars.* ISBN 978-1-591-84556-0.
- James Rickards. *The New case for Gold.* ISBN 978-0-241-24835-5.
- Dick Stroud. *The Joy of Moaning.* ISBN 9780995657731
- Mark E Thomas. *99%.* ISBN 978-1-789-54451-0
- Arthur Wise. *The Day the Queen Flew to Scotland for the Grouse Shooting* SBN 340-10770-7.

Books That Informed the Discussion:

- Matthew Brown & Rhian E. Jones. *Paint Your Town Red.* ISBN 978-1-913-46219-2.
- Gavin Esler. *How Britain Ends.* ISBN 978-1-800-24105-3.
- Steve Keen. *The New Economics.* ISBN 978-1-509-54529-2.
- Steve Keen. *Debunking Economics.* ISBN 978-1-84813-992-3.

- Jaron Lanier. *Ten arguments for Deleting your Social Media Account Right Now*. ISBN 978-1-529-11240-5.
- Quentin Letts. *Patronising Bastards*. ISBN 978-1-4721-2735-8.
- Branco Milanovic. *Global Inequality*. ISBN 978-0-674-98403-5.
- Keir Milburn. *Generation Left*. ISBN 978-1-509-53224-7.
- New Scientist. *Nothing.* Ed. J. Webb. ISBN 978-1615192052
- Peter Oborne. *The Assault on Truth*. ISBN 978-1-398-50100-3.
- Eli Pariser. *The Filter Bubble*. ISBN 978-0-241-95452-2.
- C. Northcote Parkinson. *Parkinson's Law*. ISBN 978-0-71951-0-489.
- Will Schutz. *The Human Element*. ISBN 1-55542-612-3
- Tim Slessor. *Lying in State*. ISBN 978-1-845-13030-5.
- Philip Stephens. *Britain Alone*. ISBN 978-0-571-34178-8.
- Shoshana Zuboff. *The Age of Surveillance Capitalism*. ISBN 978-1-78283-274-4.

<u>**A Thank-You**</u>

This book has been:

Written
Re-written
Re-ordered
Deduplicated
Augmented
Pruned
Revised
Summarised
Polished
Edited
Revised again
Pruned again
Repolished
Finally published

All through the good offices of Dr. David Clegg, an old school friend who has been suitably critical.

Many thanks.

2027 will be my 80th birthday when I will have been fortunate enough to have lived through a number of social and governmental changes whilst avoiding the direct conflict of a world war – there have, however, been local wars, country wars and almost wars (the Bay of Pigs for example).

As a youngster brought up in a West Yorkshire village with a slag heap at either end, I was lucky never to know real poverty; we didn't have much money and on Thursdays if mum had a few coppers left over she would buy five Woodbines; if not, she would visit Mrs. Watson's bakery, buy four stale teacakes on tick and toast them for our tea.

In 1965 I passed a few exams and went to Liverpool University for a learning; a time when anti-establishment demos were fun, seminal pop music was on the rise, and Flower-Power was at its height (and I studied tolerance to heavy metals!) I left in 1969 with an education as well as a learning.

My time in Liverpool had been paid for by the government as an exercise in developing people to help grow the country at a time when only about 5% of people made it to university and only about 3% ended up as graduates.

It's quite different today when about 50% of people become students and have to take out a loan for the privilege. This has led to a very different student attitude and a different attitude by academia who want the income.

Perhaps summarised by: 'I paid you loads of money, can I have a degree please' and academic institutions no longer failing students (politically incorrect?) but give *Deferred Passes*; I believe this is a contributor to society's gradual degeneration.

There wasn't much work in the North (during holidays I had worked as a fitter's labourer to earn a few shillings) and so I headed south for interview and found employment.

On my return from interview, I shared a carriage with a couple of southern lads, one of whom was continually peering out of the window when his companion said "why are you so intent on what's happening outside?" He received the reply "I'm looking for my first slag heap".

Such was the disparity between north and south back in the 1960s and, now back north permanently after living in the south for many years returning home occasionally to see the family, I fear this disparity is greater than ever, with real poverty in the north and the feeling of a return to the olden days I never knew the depth of, but described by Alex Niven [*The North Will Rise Again* pp.275, 276] as *'The proceeds of Victorian heavy industry were largely funnelled away from the Nort-East and into the pockets of a wealthy mine-owning class who mostly lived elsewhere'* – except, today we don't have the mines that supported a good proportion of the northern population.

During my life there have been a number of very obvious major changes which are discussed in more detail above and have been, in summary:

- Significant invention during and after the second world war, then investment in development and training – I actually got a grant to go to university, now you have to pay.
- Expansion; after graduating I went into the food industry and for five or six years was involved in new factories and commissioning plant all over the UK, industry was also benefiting from government grants.
- After the expansion and diversification we got a period of regulation, some to ensure compliance with common standards for export (we joined the EU in 1973) and some more to comply with increasing UK regulation.
- At this point I became independent, monitoring other consultants' work and joining The Richmond Group – a great opportunity to learn from competitors, take on additional methods and also broaden and deepen the services I was competent to offer.
- Then, into the new century, we entered a period of stagnation and a paucity of decision-making, exacerbated by the financial fiasco of 2008 – but a period of significant administration, reporting and bureaucracy.

- Despite this bureaucracy and stagnation, as a business consultant I had clients that tripled their net profit, some grew by over 20% p.a. compound for over ten years and others doubled production with the same number of staff in fewer hours.

From my early twenties, and the stark differences in attitude and expectation, emphasised by deep experience of both the north and the south, I still have a vision of the North rising up to reclaim the opportunity and dignity that has been incrementally eroded over the decades.

Now, on retirement, it would be easy to rest on my laurels and gently moulder; however, I think life should have purpose and so I decided to do what I could to restore some semblance of equality.

Hence this book – a follow-on to **Yorkshire, The Case For Independence** which is a feasibility study establishing that equality is actually possible (and can be achieved within a measurable number of years) – we just need a strategy to take us there and brings to reality some of the many publications telling us how unfair it all is.

As well as standing up for Yorkshire, I enjoy walking [*8 Miles to the Pub*], writing to clear loads of stuff from a softening brain [*Beyond Money*] and getting involved where I think I can contribute, whether the local social club or the County of Yorkshire.

I hope you enjoy this short book, and all comments (however scathing) will be welcome through the publisher.

Steve Mullins

March 2023